Human Variation
in Space and Time

To Margaret

ELEMENTS OF ANTHROPOLOGY
A Series of Introductions

Human Variation in Space and Time

Kenneth A. R. Kennedy

Cornell University

WM. C. BROWN COMPANY PUBLISHERS
Dubuque, Iowa

ANTHROPOLOGY SERIES

Consulting Editors

Frank Johnston
University of Pennsylvania

Henry Selby
Temple University

Contents

Preface

This book is written for people who are moved, as am I, by the wonder of man's biological diversity. With a Roman writer of the first century A.D., we recognize that

the human features and countenance, although composed of but some ten parts or little more, are so fashioned that among so many thousands of men there are no two in existence who cannot be distinguished from one another.[1]

But we shall want to go beyond this observation and ask how entire populations have evolved distinguishing physical characteristics that define *Homo sapiens* today and in the past. The fact that diversity is a property of all living things means that this phenomenon is important for survival of both individuals and populations and that mechanisms must operate in nature to ensure the perpetuation of variability in species.

In exploring the nature of human biological variation, it will be helpful to try two approaches: (1) the investigation of the historical development of ideas about human variation and (2) the analysis of these ideas in the context of how human populations are variable from one another in different parts of the world and from generation to generation.

Over the past 200 years, scholars have thought about questions of man's variation in space and time within the framework of a *race concept*. The classification of human populations into categories below the level of species has been a preoccupation of some scientists until quite recently. For this reason, if we are to understand how variation of our species is interpreted today by biologists and anthropol-

ogists, knowledge of earlier ideas on the subject is appropriate and necessary.

The parameters of space and time that describe the scope of our study are relevant, too, in observing how ideas that are of interest to us had their roots in the Greco-Roman world, later became part of the Western tradition of Europe and the Americas, and presently constitute an integral part of research on human variation that is being carried out in all parts of the world where trained investigators conduct their field work. The temporal aspect of our study applies to the evolutionary process itself that operates now and in the past. For those who can read the record of geology, paleontology, and archeology, the biological history of man is translatable as a drama wherein every individual born into the world has had a part to play.

The writing of this book has been a pleasant task and one that has made me mindful of a debt to past and contemporary scholars thinking along these same lines of finding out more about man's diversity. To my own mentor, the late Theodore D. McCown of the University of California, Berkeley, I acknowledge that awakening of a desire to discover the story of man's biological history in South Asia, my present area of field research. Through Kurt Stern and Clarence J. Glacken, both of Berkeley, I discovered the excitement of human genetics and the value of an historical orientation to all areas of scientific inquiry. Citations of the

1. Harris Rackham, trans. *Historia naturalis of Pliny the Elder* (London: Heineman, 1949), book 7, section 8.

PREFACE
Continued

many reference sources appearing in this book testify to my obligation to their authors. To select some names for special recognition would not be fair to the others left unmentioned. Miss Debbie Caro and Miss Lydia Bukowy were very helpful in assisting me with the many research details of the project. It was with the compassion, good humor, and clerical assistance of my wife that the completion of the manuscript was made possible.

1 | Importance of the Study of Human Variation

Like leaves on trees the race of man is found
Now green in youth, now withering on the ground:
Another race the following spring supplies:
They fall successive and successive rise.[1]

On the first day of class, students in my undergraduate course on Human Biological Variation were given the assignment of collecting definitions and usages of the term *race*. Later in the semester the most interesting and varied of the several hundred quotations collected were read aloud and discussed. Here are a few selections that exemplify how broadly the term race has been used. The one cited above is from the *Iliad* attributed to Homer and dated to around the eighth century B.C.

The Scottish judge Henry Home (Lord Kames) (1696-1782) wrote in an economic treatise on Ireland that

there are different races of men, and . . . these races or kinds are naturally fitted to different climates: whence we have reason to conclude, that originally each kind was placed in its proper climate, whatever change may have happened in later times by war or commerce.[2]

Madison Grant (1865-1937) was an American lawyer who defended the doctrine of Nordic supremacy. Writing at the dawn of World War I, he had this to say about racial mixture.

It must be borne in mind that the specializations which characterize the higher races are of relatively recent development, are highly unstable and when mixed with generalized or primitive characters, tend to disappear. Whether we like to admit it or not, the result of the mixture of two races, in the long run gives us a race reverting to the more ancient, generalized and primitive type. The cross between a white man and an Indian is an Indian; the cross between a white man and a Negro is a Negro; the cross between a white man and a Hindu is a Hindu; and the cross between any of the three European races and a Jew is a Jew.[3]

After denouncing the Treaty of Versailles and in preparation for his invasion of Ethiopia, the Italian dictator Benito Mussolini (1883-1945) declared, "Race! It is a feeling, not a reality."[4]

One student found this statement by Lothar G. Tirala (1886-   ), a pro-Nazi writer who dealt with the term race in a phylogenetic context.

It is a well-grounded view that it is highly probable that different human races originated in-

1. Alexander Pope, trans. *The Iliad of Homer* (New York: Macmillan, 1965), book 6, line 181.
2. Henry Home (Lord Kames), "The Political Anatomy of Ireland," in *Economic Writings*, ed. C. H. Hull (Cambridge: Cambridge University, 1899), pp. 121-231.
3. Madison Grant, *The Passing of the Great Race* (New York: Scribner's Sons, 1916), p. 15.
4. Emil Ludwig, *Talks with Mussolini* (Boston: Little, Brown, 1933), pp. 69-70.

dependently of one another and that they evolved out of different species of ape-men. . . The so-called main races of mankind are not races, but species . . . the voice of blood and race operates down to the last refinement of thought and exercises a decisive influence on the direction of thought.[5]

The Bureau of Human Betterment and Eugenics in Berlin published this statement on the eve of World War II.

This accurately expresses the racial view held by the National Socialists: that each race on earth represents an idea in the mind of God. This is just what we believe and therefore we call for a clear-cut differentiation between blood and blood, so that God's idea may not be blurred and caricatured by the half-breed.[6]

An American physician from the South who was interviewed during this same period in history by social anthropologists studying class and caste structure in our own society had this to say.

The way I look at it is this way: God didn't put the different races here to all mix and mingle so that you wouldn't know them apart. He put them here as separate races and meant them to stay that way. I don't say He put the Caucasians here to rule the world or anything like that. I don't say He put them here to be a superior race: but since they have a superior intellect and intelligence, I don't think God would want them to mingle with inferior races and lose that superiority.[7]

Soon after assuming the presidency of Argentina in 1946, Juan Perón (1895-1974) announced

for us, race is not a biological concept. For us, it is something spiritual. It constitutes a sum of the imponderables that make us what we are and impel us to be what we should be, through our origin and through our destiny. It is that which dissuades us from falling into the imitation of other communities whose natures are foreign to us. For us, race constitutes our personal seal, indefinable and irrefutable.[8]

The United States Census of Population Bureau included this statement in a report of 1960.

The concept of race, as used by the Bureau of the Census, is derived from that which is commonly accepted by the general public. It does not, therefore, reflect clear-cut differences of biological stock, and several categories obviously refer to national origin.[9]

William C. Boyd (1903-   ), an immunologist who has written on man's biological variables, has defined race as "a population which differs significantly from other human populations in regard to the frequency of one or more genes it possesses."[10]

Another eminent student of human evolution is Sherwood L. Washburn (1911-   ). He wrote that

the races of man are the result of human evolution, of the evolution of our species. . . The races are open parts of the species, and the species is a closed system. . . The evolution of races is due, according to modern genetics, to mutation, selection, migration, and genetic drift. . . Genetic theory forces the consideration of culture as a major factor in the evolution of man. We have, then, on the one hand the history of cultural systems, and finally the interrelations between the two.[11]

5. Lothar G. Tirala, *Rasse, Geist und Seele* (Munich: Lehmans Verlag, 1935).

6. Walter Gross, *Ratio-Political Foreign Correspondence* (Berlin: Bureau of Human Betterment and Eugenics, 1935).

7. Allison Davis, Burleigh Gardner, and Mary Gardner, *Deep South: a Social Anthropological Study of Caste and Class* (Chicago: University of Chicago, 1941), p. 17.

8. M. F. Ashley Montagu, *Man's Most Dangerous Myth: the Fallacy of Race*, 3rd ed. (New York: Harper and Brothers, 1952), p. 10.

9. *United States Summary, General Population Characteristics* (Washington, D.C.: United States Census of Populations, 1960), p. xiii.

10. William C. Boyd, *Population* (New York: Macmillan, 1961), p. 121.

11. Sherwood L. Washburn, "The Study of Race," *American Anthropologist* 65 (1963):521-522.

A freshman student interviewed by a member of the class at the local Rathskeller in Collegetown, Ithaca, New York, had this to say.

Race means color, man. Nothing else. If you're not black, then you're white or yellow or red or some mixed up cat. Maybe we're all a little mixed up.

The well-known writer of books on education and the history of literature, Jacques Barzun (1907-), reached this conclusion about the term *race*, placing the burden of better definitions upon geneticists.

To sum up: a satisfactory definition of race is not to be had. The formulas in common use do not really define or do not accord with the facts, so that a prudent man will suspend judgement until genetics can offer a more complete body of knowledge.[12]

Finally, we looked at a statement by Alexander Alland, Jr. (1931-), an anthropologist with interests in human adaptability and behavior. He included these ideas in the Introduction of one of his recently published books.

Population genetics proved long ago that units below the level of species could not be taken as discrete typological entities, separate in kind from other such entities. Races represented different clusters of gene frequencies and were defined as overlapping units which differed primarily in mean gene frequencies. So-called typological thinking gave way to populational thinking, but race was still seen as a useful if vague unit lying somewhere between the species and the population. More recently, biologists have questioned the utility of race altogether. Evidence from infrahuman species as well as from human populations tends to show that no successful units can be created on the subspecific level. The data have forced research on human diversity onto a new path. Classification for the sake of classification has given way to the analysis of process.[13]

Of course the purpose of this class exercise was to demonstrate that the term *race* has been defined in a number of ways, appears in diverse contexts, and shows no sign of passing out of our vocabulary. A concept that is so pervasive in the modern world is worthy of closer scrutiny as to its historical development and place in the study of human biological variation.

Contemporary anthropologists restrict the use of *race* to the study of biological variations, which occur in different frequencies in populations living today and in the past. The expressions of human diversity with which we are concerned here are essentially those that have a genetic basis. They are the traits transmitted from parents to offspring within a breeding population or by the mating of individuals from separate breeding populations of the species. Mechanisms for the transmission of cultural characters are quite different, however. We acquire knowledge of our society's customs, belief systems, languages, and many patterns of behavior by means of learning. Cultural traditions may be acquired through formal education as well as by less conscious means, as we all know from our experiences of passive observation and imitation of other people's behavior. Many of the cultural practices we acquire as members of a social group are highly symbolic and apparently arbitrary. The recognition that biological variation is of a different order of phenomena than cultural variation and that there is no scientific evidence to support an arrangement of human populations into a graded series of inferior to superior races are two important concepts anthropologists have contributed to modern thought.

Few writers in the biological sciences and anthropology would continue to apply the term *race* in contexts that are obviously political (*American* race), religious (*Jewish* race), linguistic (*Celtic* race), mythological (*Aryan* race), or economic (a race of *Arabian oil merchants*). However, the study of human variation is not the exclusive concern of anthropologists, and issues that are labeled *racial* will continue to be used by social workers, psychol-

12. Jacques Barzun, *Race: a Study in Superstition* (New York: Harper & Row, 1965), p. 16.
13. Alexander Alland, Jr., *Human Diversity* (New York: Columbia University, 1971), p. 3.

ogists, persons active in improving the quality of life for members of social minority groups and by religious leaders. In these contexts the biological limitations of the term are seldom observed, and confusion as to the significance of *race* is thereby perpetuated.

This book is being written at a time when the traditional anthropological concept of biological race is undergoing change, as Barzun and Alland indicate in the quotations you have just read. Some students of human variation have gone so far as to suggest that *race* be a word expunged from our language. Not only does it carry the burden of popular usages, but its significance as a biological concept is also under attack. We shall be tracing the origins and growth of this argument in the coming chapters.

The fact of man's biological variation is not altered or its importance diminished as a problem for investigation, whatever be the fate of the particular term used in the past to refer to research on human diversity. Through an understanding of how the concept of race emerged in our culture, how it has been altered by new approaches to the study of our species, and how cultural behavior and biological variables may interact we discover the most practical reason above all others for studying human variability—a better understanding of ourselves as individuals.

Within a framework of investigating ongoing human evolution, the scope of man's adaptive characters may be discerned. Degrees of genetic affinity between populations become measurable, and the rates and effects of evolutionary mechanisms may be assessed. Here lie significant implications for understanding the health profile of a population, particularly with respect to establishing the genetic basis for diseases and the relationship of pathologies to breeding patterns and normal standards of growth and development. Adaptability of populations to different climatic conditions, altitudes, and nutritional levels are other critical factors in the medical applications of the study of human variation. The existence of biologically variable groups of people adapting in a number of different ways to the broad spectrum of ecological settings is the anthropologist's laboratory for testing hypotheses of how man evolved specific biological adaptations.

In the study of prehistoric man, the skeletal and archeological records provide only partial data. Stanley M. Garn (1922-   ) has observed, "One of the uses of the present is to clarify the past, and so we employ living races to understand and establish fossil taxa."[14] It is possible to test various statistical measures of population affinity when applied to ancient or remnant populations. Finally, it is valuable to study variation of our species across geographical space and from past to present times in order to teach those who are confused by the claims of nationalistic and racist groups that certain populations are favored over others in the worlds of nature, politics, or religion.

For Further Reading

Baker, Paul T. "The Biological Race Concept as a Research Tool," in *Science and the Concept of Race*, ed. Margaret Mead, *et al.* New York: Columbia University, 1968, pp. 94-102. The relevance of traditional racial classifications to present-day studies of genetic distance is discussed.

Klass, Morton and Hellman, Hal *The Kinds of Mankind: an Introduction to Race and Racism.* Philadelphia: J. B. Lippincott, 1971. Chapter seventeen of this book for the high school or freshman college reader has the title *Why Study Race?*

Montagu, M. F. Ashley, ed. *Frontiers of Anthropology.* New York: G. P. Putnam's Sons, 1974. This compendium of anthropological writings by various authors of the past two centuries includes several selections dealing with the changing concept of race.

Bibliography

Birdsell, Joseph B. 1975. *Human Evolution: an Introduction to the New Physical Anthropology.* Chicago: Rand McNally.

Garn, Stanley M., ed. 1960. *Readings on Race.* Springfield, Ill.: Charles C. Thomas.

UNESCO 1961. *The Race Question in Modern Science: Race and Science.* New York: Columbia University. (Articles by eleven authors.)

14. Stanley M. Garn, *Human Races*, 3rd ed. (Springfield, Ill.: Charles C. Thomas, 1971), p. 185.

2 | Of Men and Monsters

ETHNOCENTRISM AND RACISM

About half of the fifty States of the Union have names of native American origin. While some are descriptive of geographical features—Mississippi from the Algonkian for *great water* or Arizona from the Papago for *small springs*—other state names are derived from tribal designations that native inhabitants of a region gave to themselves or to their neighbors. Oklahoma means *the red people* in the Chactaw language. In the Illinek dialect Illinois can be translated as *the men* or *the true people.* The Dakotas are rendered in Santee Sioux as *allies,* which is close to a literal translation of the name given by a group of tribes in Texas to themselves and their confederates. The term used by a population to designate itself may not be the same as that used by nonallied groups outside a territory. Eskimo, meaning *eaters of raw flesh,* is a derogatory name given by Algonkian Indians to those Arctic people who call themselves the Insuit, or simply *the men.* Names for groups outside the category *we* mean strangers, barbarians, or even monsters. Anthropologists have discovered from their worldwide investigations of human populations that these practices just described are common.

An individual's sense of identity with the particular population in which he was raised is based upon his acceptance of those distinctive features of habitat, custom, language, and familiar physical appearances of other members of his group. These are one's standards of normalcy. The corollary of this attitude is that other human groups, particularly those inhabiting geographical areas outside the boundaries of one's home range whose behavioral and physical characteristics are different, are therefore less perfect expressions of humanity than the *we the people,* the folk at home. This tendency to regard foreign groups of people with disfavor and to judge them according to the standards of one's own society fosters a habit of mind called *ethnocentrism.* The term *folk racism* is also used to indicate the belief that the standards of one's own ethnic group are superior.

Ethnocentrism is a universal concept. However, those particular attitudes of group loyalty and superiority that are encountered in cross-cultural surveys are notions every individual acquires through learning and as a member of his social group. Whatever basis there may be for the existence of inborn tendencies in man for aggressive defense of territory, an argument in vogue today within the scientific community[1] and with lay writers of popular anthropology,[2] the weight of ethnographic evidence gathered so far falls on the

1. Alexander Alland, *The Human Imperative* (New York: Columbia University, 1972): Konrad Lorenz, *On Aggression* (New York: Harcourt Brace, 1966); Lional Tiger, *Men in Groups* (New York: Random House, 1969).

2. Robert Ardrey, *The Territorial Imperative* (New York: Dell, 1966).

side of those who hold ethnocentric biases to be the products of one's cultural background.

Emotional bonds that unite an individual to his ethnic group have important biological implications. Cases are known of some human populations undergoing too rapid a degree of cultural change with the result that their traditional institution become seriously threatened. Loss of a personal self-respect and a positive ethnic identity are an ultimate danger, especially when new behavior patterns are imposed that cannot be integrated satisfactorily into the framework of the older cultural norms. Biological as well as cultural extinction of the affected population may be the result. Examples of this tragic situation are legion: many native American populations, the aborigines of Tasmania, the hill tribes of South Asia. Other populations faced with acculturation by association with outside groups have succeeded in preserving their sense of ethnic identity and continue as biological populations. In this context we think of the Navaho and Cherokee peoples, the Berber nomads of North Africa, and enclaves of Celtic-speaking peoples in western Europe. In these latter cases, cultural adaptability was the deciding factor in their biological survival.

While ethnocentrism is found in all societies, in Europe and America it assumed the form of *racism* when reasons of a specific kind were given to explain and prove how persons of European descent were innately superior to persons of other backgrounds. This point was argued on the premise that cultural and biological traits are correlated. In the early part of the nineteenth century, so-called scientific reasons were put forward by a number of Western writers to support ethnocentric biases. The origins of racism date to that time.[3] Value judgements concerning differences of custom and physique between human populations became superimposed upon classifications of the species into racial categories, and the validity of a hierarchy was assumed to be scientifically demonstrable. The division of mankind into races is not the essence of racism. Rather it is the practice of misapplying the data of scientific inquiry about human diversity in such a way that a justification for exploiting and discriminating against particular populations becomes accepted as a social sanction. Racism is nonadaptive for humanity, whatever short-term goals may be realized by individuals asserting dominance over a specific group of people. This attitude inhibits communication between populations and a fair sharing of the earth's products in an ever-contracting world community. Tactics of terror and genocide are the inevitable consequences of racist propaganda.

It is unfortunate that many people do not understand the distinction between racism and the objective scientific study of human groups by investigators seeking to explain how mankind evolved the myriad adaptive variations characteristic of *Homo sapiens* today and in the past. Discoveries of hitherto unknown biological variables are being announced all the time by laboratory researchers and by medical and anthropological personnel in the field. Only a very incurious person would not wonder about the origins, geographical distribution, and adaptive significance of the human differences in blood types, skin pigmentation, sensitivity to substances in foods and drugs, stature and body form, rates of growth and development, and capacities to resist certain diseases. When did these and literally thousands of other biological characters come into existence? What are the evolutionary histories of those biological traits found in high frequency in our species today? Why are other traits group-specific (i.e., found only in one or a few populations)?

Whether one accepts the traditional classifications of mankind into races or not, the fact of human diversity is indisputable and merits continuing scientific research. Because this field of inquiry has for so long a time been associated with the thesis that races are real and natural divisions of our species, it has become associated with the term *racial anthropology*. However, with the erosion of the race concept during the past few years, contemporary students of man's biological variation would prefer to be called *population geneticists* or students of human adaptive variability. The term *race* occurs less frequently today in college course titles when instruction is given by anthropologists, but it continues to appear in courses and

3. M. F. Ashley Montagu, *The Idea of Race* (Lincoln: University of Nebraska, 1965).

texts dealing with sociology and *race relations* in other areas of the social sciences where the social implications of racism are concerned.[4]

ATTITUDES IN ANTIQUITY TOWARDS HUMAN DIFFERENCES

There have always been some people who recognized the fallacy of ethnocentric thinking, even before the time when anthropologists made it a part of their professional business to analyse the concept. Certain ancient Greeks appreciated the adaptive aspects of their own ethnocentricity as an indicator of social and political well-being. But they saw, too, that those peoples living beyond the pale of Greek civilization—the uncouth barbarians —held the same good opinion of themselves as did respectable citizens of a Greek city-state. This ironical circumstance was discussed by the historian Herodotus (484?-425 B.C.), a native of Halicarnassus in Asia Minor, who had traveled over much of the known world of the fifth century B.C. He has been hailed as the *father of anthropology*, although he has been held responsible as well for the paternity of history, journalism, and tourism! In his account of the political struggle of Persians and Greeks, Herodotus wrote that

if the whole human race were given a free field and were instructed to choose out the best laws from all the laws in existence, after due consideration they would each choose their own laws—so convinced are they respectively of the immeasurable superiority of their own.[5]

The ethnocentric thinking of ancient Greeks surpassed their pride of citizenship as an Athenian or an Ithacan to encompass the very spirit of Hellenic civilization itself. The philosopher Isocrates (436-338 B.C.) expressed this point of view when he wrote

so far has Athens outdistanced the rest of mankind in thought and in speech that her pupils have become the teachers of the rest of the world; and she has brought it about that the name of *Hellenes* is applied rather to those who share our culture than to those who share a common blood.[6]

This is hardly an expression of that form of racism that appears two thousand years later in the western part of Europe. Isocrates is stating that the cultural duality of Greeks and non-Greeks (barbarians) could be dissolved given the Hellenization of those people living beyond the pale. A universal brotherhood of man was a possibility because individuals could transcend the behavioral patterns they had acquired as members of their local community and become subjects under a single social law.

Barbarians included all foreigners, be these cultivated Orientals, rustic illiterates, or slaves. The majority of slaves came from foreign parts. Negative attitudes about non-Greeks were engendered by political circumstances; and claims were made that slavery was a *natural* condition for barbarous races who were servile by temperament and not naturally free people, as were their Greek masters. Even the Roman conquerors of Greece and her colonial outposts in remote parts of Africa and Asia were quick to acknowledge their cultural debt to the vanquished, easily assuming Greek ethnocentric concepts themselves as they expanded their political influence.[7] A spirit of

4. Gordon Allport, *The Nature of Prejudice* (Cambridge: Addison-Wesley, 1953); Pierre van den Berghe, *Race and Racism* (New York: John Wiley and Sons, 1967); Jean Finot, *Race Prejudice* (New York: E. P. Dutton, 1905); Joseph S. Himes, *Racial and Ethnic Relations* (Dubuque, Iowa: Wm. C. Brown Company Publishers, 1974); John S. Haller, *Outcasts From Evolution* (Urbana: University of Illinois, 1971); Kenneth M. Ludmerer, *Genetics and American Society* (Baltimore: Johns Hopkins University, 1972); Philip Mason, *Patterns of Dominance* (London: Oxford University, 1970); M. F. Ashley Montagu, *Race, Science and Humanity* (New York: Van Nostrand, 1963); John Oakesmith, *Race and Nationality* (New York: F. A. Stokes, 1919); Louis Ruchames, ed. *Racial Thought in America* (Amherst: University of Massachusetts, 1969); and Louis L. Snyder, *A History of Modern Ethnic Theories* (New York: Longmans, Green, 1939).

5. Arnold J. Toynbee, *Greek Historical Thought: from Homer to the Age of Heraclius* (New York: American Library, 1952), p. 141.

6. Olaus Gigon, ed. *Orationes selectal accedit Isocrates Panegricus* (Bern: A Francke, 1944).

7. Greeks accorded the same respect to the Egyptians, even tracing the roots of their religions, philosophies, and legal codes to this earlier established civilization. Biological factors played no part in this often exaggerated claim of cultural indebtedness.

tolerance and cultural relativism prevailed in antiquity. However the human status of the fabled monstrous tribes reputed to live along the borders of the known world was questioned.

Travelers of the Greco-Roman world frequently reported that the foreign peoples they encountered could be distinguished from one another and from Greeks by some physical characters. Stature, skin and hair pigmentation, and the form of the hair were features noted most often. These are, after all, the physical variables that are immediately obvious to any observer. The same features were of interest to Egyptian artists of the fourteenth century B.C. whose tomb paintings represent Semites, Negroes, Lybians, and African pygmies. Members of these populations are distinguished as much by their characteristic physical features as they are by their costumes. Travelers of the ancient world also came upon tribes who practiced head deformation by means of cradling and head-binding procedures, and this curiosity was recorded too. Not infrequently, bodily deformations were thought to be inherited traits although initiated, perhaps, by cultural practices. The often seen tribal name of *Macrocephali* refers in some cases to barbarians who deformed their heads. An assymetrical or enlarged head was considered unesthetic according to Greek standards of beauty.

The customs of barbarians were given far more attention than were their physical characters. Laws, rituals of death and burial, marriage rites, religious customs, habitations, and modes of dress held particular interest in the minds of ancient writers. Diet, too, was a criterion of culture, hence the identification of some tribes bordering the Red Sea and Indian Ocean as Ichthyophagi (fish-eaters), Chelonophagi (turtle-eaters), and Spermatophagi (seed-eaters). The Anthropophagi (man-eaters or cannibals) were a popular topic of discussion by persons who had traveled to the nether regions. But beyond these descriptions, no attempt was made to classify humanity on the basis of custom, language, or physique.[8]

This brings us back to Herodotus whose journeys took him from Iran to Italy and from the coast of the Black Sea to the area of Assuan on the Nile. In describing the fifty or so tribes he visited or heard about from neighboring communities, Herodotus sought to free himself of ethnocentric bias and moral judgement and to be skeptical of hearsay accounts. Apart from some lapses of gullibility regarding the monstrous tribes in the hinterlands, he was for the most part successful in this effort at objective reporting. His *History* is a unique book for these reasons. It is the fullest anthropological study that has come down to us from this early period.[9]

In distinguishing one tribe from another, Herodotus observed customs and languages, his notes on physical differences being interspersed among other descriptive details. He was unwilling to give biological variables any more attention than he thought they deserved, since he did not consider them fundamental in any way to his account of human diversity. He knew that separate tribes might share similar physical features yet possess quite distinct languages and arts. For example, he compared the dark-skinned and curly-haired inhabitants of Egypt and Colchis (Soviet Republic of Georgia) with other people far removed from them geographically who, he reported, also had swarthy skins and curly hair, but spoke different tongues and practiced other arts. We shall find little in Herodotus's *History* about the origins of particular tribes, for he seems to have been uninterested in this problem, seldom recording for us their own legends and claims of descent. Where an exception occurs, as in his account of the tradition of a tribe on the Danube that its ethnic origins were in Persia, the claim is left unchallenged. In a world of great ethnic diversity, the possibility of a migration of this scope would not be considered out of the question by that energetic traveler.

Other ancient scholars were interested in the question of how human variation came about. The Homeric myths of cosmic creation and human origins were no longer interpreted literally by educated persons of the time when Herodotus was undertaking his adventures in

8. Edward E. Sikes, *The Anthropology of the Greeks* (London: David Nutt, 1914).

9. George Rawlinson, trans. *Historiae of Herodotus* (New York: E. P. Dutton, 1910).

distant places, although allegorical interpretations of myths were popular. Nevertheless, it is within this mythological tradition that we discern the earliest efforts of Western man to deal with the fact of human variation. Three themes are present in accounts ascribed to Homer are to other ancient mythologists: (1) different human groups arose from primal pairs of parents in localities where their descendants live today; (2) mankind had a single creation through the act of a deity, differences between human groups developing after this supernatural event from influences of the natural environment; (3) mankind arose as a result of spontaneous generation, sometimes by the will of a god or hero who conjured up citizens in the establishment of a new city, at other times to provide troops for an army. According to this latter motif, the hero Cadmus populated Thebes by sewing the teeth of a serpent into the ground. Thus human variations might be accounted for by a number of separate en masse creations of populations, individuals springing up from serpent's teeth, seeds, or from similar processes.

Dismissing these explanations of human variation as so many fairy tales, Herodotus came close to offering an historical interpretation of human diversity. He assumed that habitual cultural practices affecting the body, such as the custom of head deformation, might become acquired permanently. He looked to the physical environment as the determinant of other physical features. But beyond some mention of tribal migrations and observing that every group he visited had some account of its origin, Herodotus did not become involved with the question of ethnic differences in a historical context. This is a curious omission in the light of the traditional Greek division of time into Five Ages. According to this chronology, man has deteriorated from his original perfect state as a child of the Golden Age to the less felicitous creature he is today through a series of historical stages identified as the Age of Silver, Age of Bronze, Age of Heroes, and finally the Age of Iron (the present day).[10]

Closely linked to these early speculations about human variation were philosophical efforts to rationalize how man came into being and to reconstruct the nature of his primeval way of life. While borrowing some elements of mythological traditions, Greek *cosmologists,* writing about the origin and nature of the universe, and *primitivists,* writing about man's early lifeways, sought to find answers by means of reasoned arguments rather than with exclusive reference to Homer and founders of mystic cults. We might hesitate to call these early thinkers *scientists,* for they did not collect and organize their knowledge in any systematic way nor develop theories based upon empirical evidence. However, they were involved with the exploratory adventure of finding new answers to ancient questions about the natural world without recourse to supernatural explanations. This is the essence of scientific method, and such an approach was possible because of the freedom of thought that prevailed in ancient Greece. Indeed, without any orthodox system of beliefs regarding man's origin, antiquity, and place in nature and in the absence of a sacred text against which heretical speculation had to find its measure of social sanctioning, a number of different theories about man could be proposed and tolerated.

Another element of this liberal climate of inquiry about man lies in the ancient view of time as a cyclical process. It was thought that one world was succeeded by another, the human inhabitants of each one passing through identical stages from a Golden Age to an Iron Age. As man's morality and the phenomena of nature descended together toward a nadir of degeneration, a worn-out world would end through a catastrophic debacle. A new world would commence by a timely supernatural intervention, thus bringing the dawn of yet another Golden Age. In this context of a cyclical succession of worlds, all phenomena and events were eternally repetitive. Man could not escape this process, which demonstrated perpetual orderliness in cosmic history.

10. In this classification of time into the Five Ages, we perceive the beginnings of a historical approach to the study of human variation. The concept is ascribed to the poet Hesiod who lived in the eighth century B.C., and ancient writers elaborated upon his teachings. They wondered if mankind had survived each of these ages as a population continuum or if a separate creation of humanity marked the onset of each new age.

While man was not elevated to a special place in creation, his capacity for rational thought and his acquisition of the arts of civilized life meant to certain Greek thinkers that man's early history lay outside the limits of mythological explanation. There developed a strong desire to account for cultural and biological diversities in man along the same lines of reasoned argument that were being applied to problems of the structure of the physical universe. The atomic theory of matter was one of several efforts to account for the essence and diversity of the material universe.

In the seaport town of Miletus in Asia Minor lived a philosopher by the name of Anaximander (611-547 B.C.). He made the suggestion that life had its origin under conditions of moisture. Successful life forms gradually adapted to dried terrestrial habitats when the sun evaporated the primeval environment. Creatures that could not adapt to these progressively more arid conditions became extinct, while other creatures managed to survive and procreate. Anaximander did not exempt man from this creative process, but he decided that the first human beings must have spent their infancies in the protective bodies of fishes, only venturing forth to meet the challenges of existence on dry land at puberty. At some later time, man became completely terrestrial and self-nurturing, his success being dependent upon his ability to adapt to various environments. Moisture and heat were thought to be powerful, generative catalysts by the ancients who assumed that creatures could arise spontaneously from river mud that was warmed and dried by the sun.

The eccentric philosopher Empedocles (fifth century B.C.), who claimed to possess divine powers and whom legend reports as hurling himself into the crater of Mount Etna to demonstrate his godlike capability of a sudden disappearance, offered the following theory to his students. Parts of animals arose spontaneously from the earth such that for a period of time eyes in want of foreheads rolled about freely while arms scrambled along devoid of shoulders. Then some of these parts became united at random, thus producing impossible and monstrous combinations. However, a number of fortuitous assemblages of corporeal elements arose from the lands and waters and were capable of surviving. Among the latter, some had acquired sexual organs and their propagation was assured. Man was one of these suitably adapted creatures.

Anaximander and Empedocles thought that the time of man's origin was synchronous with that of other living things, Anaximander making the point that man excels the animals only in a capacity for reason and for learning the requirements of civilized life. These traits were prerequisite to increasing degrees of human diversity, which resulted from man's acquisition of the rudiments of culture. The exact nature of man's primeval way of life was debated by those philosophers we call the primitivists. Some of them held that the Golden Age was a time of insouciant contentment and luxury when man maintained himself in a beneficent state of equilibrium with nature. Others emphasized the harshness and stressful qualities of man's early history, which was blessed only by the practice of stoical virtues. There was more general agreement that as man progressed from a nomadic lifeway to a more sedentary commitment to agriculture and husbandry, he bore the responsibilities and evils of property ownership. These concerns led to greed and warfare. Inevitable changes continued to the present Age of Iron with all its woes, despite efforts of mankind to regulate conduct by a formulation of laws and political systems. The Roman poet Lucretius (96?-?55 B.C.) wrote a detailed account of man's primeval state of nature in his work *Of the Nature of Things*.[11] Lucretius touches upon a basic tenet of ancient thought, which was later to be absorbed into Christian theology: change and diversity in the affairs of men had effects that were deleterious. But other ancient primitivists saw cultural changes as progressive, since man had the capacity to learn and thus improve his lot.

In later antiquity the idea prevailed that life for early man had been brutish and miserable, but as early as the fifth century B.C. the Hippocratic treatise *On Ancient Medicine* already contains this premise, adding that without sufficient knowledge of the healing arts, primeval man chronically suffered from

11. W.H.S. Rouse, trans. *De rerum natura of Lucretius* (Cambridge: Harvard University, 1937).

diseases and indigestion![12] This situation was relieved only with the procurement of fire, the skills of food production and animal domestication, and the evolution of social laws. The reputed author of this work was a native of the island of Cos, lying off the coast of Anatolia (Turkey). Hippocrates (460?-?377 B.C.) wrote another treatise—*On Air, Water and Places*—in which he dealt specifically with the possible causes of human population differences in the dimensions of space and time.[13]

He observed that man was sensitive to changes of both the natural and social environments. He ascribed human biological and psychological adaptability to the influence of persistent customs, geography, and climate. Circumstances of man's origins were not of any particular concern to Hippocrates. He assumed that cultural practices could become inherited, as we may see from his description of the Phasians, a tribe living in a portion of Asia that today lies in the Soviet Republic of Georgia.

That country is marshy and warm and well watered and thickly clothed with vegetation, and there is heavy and violent rainfall there at all seasons. The habitat of its men is in the marshes, and their houses are of wood and rushes ingeniously erected in the water, and they do but little walking to and from town and market, but they sail to and fro in dug-out canoes. For there are numerous artificial canals. The waters they drink are warm and stagnant and putrified by the sun, and replenished by the rains. The Phasis itself, too, is the most stagnant of rivers, and of the gentlest current. And the fruits which grow there are all unwholesome, for they are effeminated and flabby by reason of the abundance of water. And that is why they do not ripen fully. And much mist envelops the country as a result of the water. For just these reasons the Phasians have their bodily forms different from those of all other men. For in stature they are tall, in breadth they are excessively broad, and no joint or vein is to be seen upon them. Their complexion is yellow as if they had the jaundice. Their voice is the deepest of all men's because their atmosphere is not clear but foggy and moist. As for bodily exertion they are naturally somewhat disinclined.[14]

Concerning the Macrocephali, Hippocrates notes again his conviction that acquired characteristics may become inherited.

In the beginning it was their custom which was chiefly responsible for the length of their head, but their mode of growth too reinforces this custom. For they are regarded as best bred those who have the longest head. . . At the beginning, the practice (of head-binding) itself had the result that their mode of growth was of this kind. But as time went on, it came to be inbred so that their law was no longer compulsory.[15]

Explaining human variation on the basis of environmental determinants was done by later writers too, and in some respects this thesis of Hippocrates's continued to seem a reasonable one to men of learning until the discovery of genetic principles at the end of the nineteenth century.

Before concluding this discussion of ancient Greek thought concerning human origins and diversity, two important concepts of pre-Christian philosophy should be noted. Both ideas survived until modern times and had a profound influence upon early scientific theories about human variation.

The first concept has to do with the notion that the world we perceive through our senses or learn about from accounts of other sentient human beings is an imperfect illusion of an ideal world that exists in the mind of a Supreme Being. Perhaps you are familiar already with Plato's (427?-347 B.C.) theory of the world of appearances and the world of ideas. He describes this in the beautiful allegory of the play of shadows on a cave wall.[16] The phenomena of nature we perceive are compared to unsubstantial apparitions, which distortedly represent those true formal entities

12. William H. S. Jones, trans. *Works of Hippocrates* (Cambridge: Harvard University, 1923).

13. Ibid.

14. John L. Myres, "Herodotus and Anthropology," in *Anthropology and the Classics*, ed. R.R. Marett (Oxford: Clarendon, 1908), pp. 146-147.

15. Ibid.

16. Francis M. Cornford, trans. *The Republic of Plato* (New York: Oxford University, 1945), pp. 227-235.

that furnish the mind of the Deity and which the dedicated philosopher can be trained to discern for himself. In this conceptual framework, the book you are holding would be a mere shadow of the form of *The Book* in the real world of ideas. Tabbies, Persians, Siamese, Manx, and Angoras are all illusive expressions of the *Absolute Cat.* So with human beings: Plato, while a man, is one possible expression of *Mankind.* With groups of people, variations between individuals and intergroup variations were of less interest to a philosopher of Plato's Academy than was the preoccupation with the idea of *Humanity,* the reality. Only unphilosophical minds would focus upon the distorted appearances of the phenomena of the sentient reality. Given these precepts, which were widely held in the ancient world, is it any wonder that a study of the causes of human variation held a minor place in scholarly endeavor? Of those philosophers who did not accept Plato's view of the world, the Epicurians and Stoics argued that the real world was the mechanistic one understood, albeit incompletely, through our senses. The atomic theory of nature dealt with this world of experiences.

The second concept, also discussed by Plato but not original with him, has to do with the organization of natural phenomena into a graded series. Organic elements were set into a conceptual model called a *chain of being.* Contained here is the assumption that since the Creator is beneficent, He could not restrict himself to the creation of certain phenomena to the exclusion of other potential existents. The physical universe is an exhaustive replica of the real world of ideas that had a single creation, although the illusive world of appearances is cyclical. This is not an evolutionary organization of nature, for existing things could become neither transformed nor extinct. The completeness of the universe was an inevitable product of a virtuous Creator, and the idea associated with this quality is called the *principle of plentitude.*[17]

Aristotle (384-322 B.C.), for twenty years a student of Plato's and later the tutor to Alexander the Great, questioned the assumption that all things must by necessity exist. But Aristotle adopted the idea of the ladder of being, adding that if living things were to be classified with reference to some specific attribute, then a linear series would become obvious. In a series of this kind, continuity would prevail, the properties of one group of animals shading imperceptibly with those at adjacent positions along the scale. In short, clear-cut divisions between living things could not occur. To this *principle of continuity* Aristotle added the *principle of linear gradation,* also called the *Scala naturae.* While recognizing that classifications contained an element of arbitrariness as a consequence of human bias, Aristotle went on to suggest that living things could be arranged in a graded series according to some criterion, be this the presence of a nutritive fluid in the body, body size, longevity, or some other variable property. Because of differences in degree of development and intensity of expression of any of these or other properties, creatures of the same kind (what we would call *species* today) possess qualities of variability. It was the task of the student of living nature to penetrate the confusions of variability and discern the *type* (i.e., the concept that most closely approximates the ideal form of which individual animals are mere manifestations). Individuals exhibit in their physical characters and behaviors varying expressions of the true form or idea of their group. If these variations can be transcended, the type will be discernible.

Some eleven grades of creatures were proposed by Aristotle. He placed mankind at the top of the scale and barely existing forms of primitive life were set at the bottom. This model of nature based upon the principles of plentitude, continuity, and linear gradation with living things arranged along an infinite hierarchical order of links from single to complex forms was the concept that complemented the Platonic view of idealized forms. Variability was regarded as a property of the world of appearances, not the object of higher philosophical speculation. This bias was perpetuated in the mainstream of biology and anthropology until the time of Charles Darwin, who demonstrated how important an awareness of variability was to the under-

17. Arthur O. Lovejoy, *The Great Chain of Being: a Study of the History of an Idea* (Cambridge: Harvard University, 1936).

standing of the evolutionary history of plants and animals.

The expansion of Roman influence in the later part of antiquity brought little that was new to speculations about human variation, even though the borders of the known world became extended considerably beyond the spheres of Greek influence. The Hellenic intellectual heritage was preserved by the Romans, travelers and scribes elaborating upon the tales of monstrous tribes handed down to them by Greek authors. The popular interest in foreign peoples with bazaar customs and hideous aspects led the soldier and statesman Pliny the Elder (23-79 A.D.) to compile an extensive encyclopedia—the *Historia naturalis*.[18] Combining notes from his diary of travels and the accounts of earlier writers, Pliny set about to describe all known tribes and monstrous halfmen in epithetic form. Here is an example of his work.

In Africa, for example, there were the cave dwellers, who lived on the flesh of snakes, and being voiceless made only squeaking noises. There were the Garamentes, who devoid of marriage rites, lived with their women promiscuously. There were also the Augilles, who worshipped the powers of the underworld, the Gamphastes, who went naked, and refrained from battle and avoided foreigners; the headless Blemmyae, with their eyes and mouthes in their chests; the Satyrs, who, except for their shape, had nothing of ordinary humanity about them; the Strapfoots, with

18. Harris Rackham, trans. *Historia naturalis of Pliny the Elder* (London: Heineman, 1949).

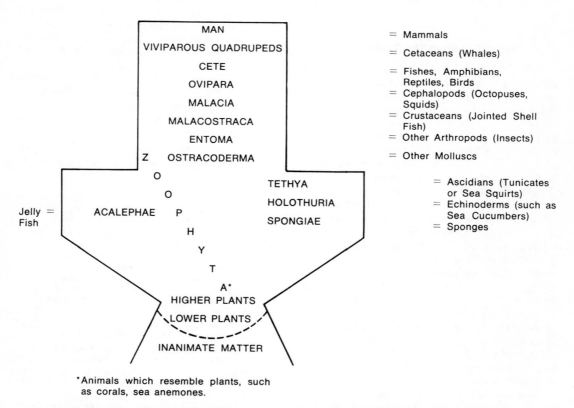

FIGURE 2.1. The **Scala Naturae** or Ladder of Being, according to descriptions of Aristotle.

feet like leather thongs, whose nature it was to crawl rather than walk.[19]

After examining four volumes on this subject, out of a collection of thirty-seven volumes of Pliny's encyclopedia, one yearns for a Roman Herodotus! But instead we come across a number of imitators of the Roman statesman, all of whom seem preoccupied with sensationalism and are devoid of curiosity about the reliability of the references cited for ancient authors.[20] It is only with certain official reports prepared for the imperial government that more factual reporting appears, as with Tacitus's (55?-117 A.D.) treatise *Concerning the Geography, the Manners and Customs of the Tribes of Germany,* which appeared in 98 A.D.[21] This brings us to the Christian era where human variation was interpreted quite differently than it had been in earlier times, yet with many ancient elements of thought preserved.

THE JUDEO-CHRISTIAN TRADITION

Following the conversion to Christianity of the Roman emperor Constantine (280?-337), when this religion was established as the official one of the empire, certain pagan concepts about nature were declared heretical. Elements of Jewish tradition already adopted by the early Christians had replaced these. For example, the notion of a cyclical world of illusive perception was incompatible with the dogma of a single creation of a unique world where every human being worked out his salvation as best he could through a dependence upon the sacraments and teachings of the church. To Christians, the advent of Christ, the Atonement, and the final Day of Judgement found no place in a cyclical system. Cycles became relevant only to speculations about the movements of celestial bodies and as allegorical references to the cycle of life. History was linear and purposeful. Nor could local creation myths, the doctrine of the Five Ages, and certain elements of pagan primitivism be tolerated side by side an acceptance of events detailed in Genesis.[22]

However, other elements of ancient thought were incorporated into Christianity. It was the goal of the early church fathers to amalgamate the prestigious pagan literature with the tenets of Judaism and Christianity wherever doctrinal conflict could be circumvented. The idea of a ladder of life did not contradict Christian teachings, and Augustine (354-430), bishop of Hippo in North Africa, regarded it as an acceptable explanation for the existence of inequalities in the universe that "if all things were equal, all things would not be."[23]

The concept of a ladder of life allowed a place in nature for all of the varieties of Adam's descendants, including the legendary monstrous tribes who, if related to Adam, were merely those human beings of greatest depravity whose position on the ladder fell below that of enlightened men. It was well after the close of the Middle Ages before attempts were made to formalize the ladder of life into a hierarchy of specific human groups, as Aristotle's eleven grades were preserved with only minor modifications until the Renaissance. Like the ancient Greeks, the medieval Christians divided the world's populations into two major groups, but to the latter the barbarians were more properly held to be all non-Christians (i.e., the pagans).

Even the theory of spontaneous generation was allowed to survive beside the biblical account of creation, although a phenomenon relevant only to those living things far below man in the ladder of life. Augustine wrote that germinative seeds exist both within living plants and animals as well as in the elements

19. Margaret T. Hodgen, *Early Anthropology in the Sixteenth and Seventeenth Centuries* (Philadelphia: University of Pennsylvania, 1964), pp. 38-39.

20. Pliny the Elder was another eccentric writer of antiquity who, like Empedocles, met his end in connection with a volcano. In the case of the Roman, the mountain was Vesuvius whose sulphurous fumes and rain of hot ashes overwhelmed Pliny and his sailing companions in a boat in the Bay of Naples when Pliny insisted that they sail closer and closer to the site of the eruption!

21. Moses Hadus, trans. *The Complete Works of Tacitus* (New York: Modern Library, 1942).

22. A reading of the first eleven chapters of Genesis, preferably of the King James Version, is essential for an understanding of the tradition of man's origins and early lifeway that has dominated Western thought for centuries.

23. George E. McCraken, trans. *De civitate dei of Augustine* (Cambridge: Harvard University, 1957).

FIGURE 2.2. The Chain of Being. From Raymond Lull's **Liber de ascensu et descensu intellectus,** 1512.

of nature. These latter seeds had the capacity to become viable under certain environmental conditions.

The Greek idea that environmental and social disruptions are deleterious because they stand to provoke changes of degenerative nature was also compatible with a Christian interpretation of the events of man's early way of life, as recorded in Genesis. Judeo-Christian primitivism pivots upon three circumstances that were thought to account for man's present state of diversity in custom, language, and bodily form.

First, there is the termination of the harmonious balance of man and nature, which Adam and his spouse precipitated when they ate of the fruit of the Tree of Knowledge of Good and Evil. Following their expulsion from Eden, they labored for survival in a harsh land. As though matters were not bad enough, the murder of one son, Abel, by his brother, Cain, forced the departure of the culprit to the land of Nod where he brought forth his own line. Cain's generation was distinguished from that

of his parents by the practice of polygamy, invention of musical instruments, and the working of metals. It was through a third son, Seth, that the Adamic line was continued.

The second disruptive phase of the Judeo-Christian tradition finds its setting in a densely populated world that is troubled by the moral misconduct of its human inhabitants. Only Noah, a descendant of Seth, and his immediate family are deemed worthy to survive a total deluge that comes to drown all creatures, save those the Noah family can drive into the ark. After ten months of waiting out the flood, all passengers return to dry land. But a family disagreement and Noah's death forces the three sons of the patriarch to leave home and settle in distant lands. Ham, who is cursed by his father on suspicion of having shown disrespect, became the founder of the peoples of Egypt, Ethiopia, Punt (Somali coast?), and Canaan (Israel). Japheth fathered the Cimmerians (Crimeans), Magogs (people of Turkey?), Medes (people of Media, a country south of the Caspian Sea in northwestern Iran), and Ionians (people on the western coast of Asia Minor). Shem's descendants were the Elamites (people living east of Babylonia and north of the Persian Gulf in Iran and Iraq), Assyrians (people living between the Tigris and Euphrates Rivers in Iraq), Lydians (people along the western coast of Asia Minor and eastward into interior Turkey), and the people of Aram (Syria).

The final phase of the sacred history of human diversity transpired at Babel when tribes gathered to erect a tower toward heaven as a security measure against the contingency of another deluge. Divine intervention brought a halt to this building project when those tribes, which shared a common tongue, suddenly began speaking languages that were mutually unintelligible. The abandonment of construction at Babel meant that mankind could never again be united by a common tradition. When Abraham began his journey from Ur, he entered a world of irreconcilable differences of customs, languages, and lifeways. To this account, the Church Fathers and their scholarly successors of the Middle Ages observed that variation was a continuing process through the influences of environmental pressures. Human diversity could be interpreted only as a consequence of moral decline. The invention of the arts of civilization, so positive a sign of man's uniqueness to many Greek philosophers, was viewed by Christian theologians as simply a further incentive to human degeneration.

The Middle Ages offer us little that is ethnologically innovative, writers, of this period preferring to perpetuate and embellish the stories of foreign peoples and monstrous halfmen handed down from antiquity. Even these accounts became distorted through careless copying and outrageous exaggeration, with the result that inhabitants of Africa and Asia could no longer be identified with accuracy in cross-reference to earlier reports. No account was taken of demographic changes transpiring over time, as it was assumed that tribes occupying areas where earlier sources reported them to be would still be living there. Some of this lore became incorporated into encyclopedias, which were modeled after the work of Pliny the Elder. These medieval manuscripts served to educate the small group of literate elite. Travelers who came into direct contact with non-European peoples seldom prepared descriptions of any anthropological significance. Missionaries, pilgrims, and merchants were not exceptions to this situation. The adventures of Marco Polo (1254?-?1324), while entertaining, cannot compare to the critical records of Herodotus in their attention to details of foreign customs and in their skepticism of hearsay reports.[24]

Along with this indifference to adding to the store of classical knowledge about human variation, an educated person of the early Middle Ages was likely to hold the notion that all descendants of Adam lived in the northern temperate zone. Presumably this was the geographical region of man's origin. The areas beyond the equator—the antipodes—were thought to be uninhabited by human beings, and medieval geographers added the detail that a fiery barrier prevented movement of Adam's descendants to the edge of the flat earth. If the antipodes *were* inhabited, its creatures could not be derived from Adam's line. Perhaps the anthropomorphic monsters of ancient legend lived beyond the equator. This brings to light an interesting element in the history of the study of human variation. Chris-

tian writers could accept a belief in a high degree of diversity in man as a descendant of Adam, but they rejected as human any creature whatever its *manlike appearance* if its affinity to our noble progenitor were in doubt.

The dogma that all true men are descendants of a single set of parents is called *monogenesis*. The heretical argument that mankind may have had multiple sets of primal parents is called *polygenesis*, a theory to which Augustine added his condemnation in his book *The City of God Against the Pagans*. In discussing the habitation of the antipodes, he wrote:

Whereas they fable of a people that inhabit that land where the sun riseth, when it setteth with us and go with their feet towards us, it is incredible. . . It were too absurd to say, that men might sail over that huge ocean, and go inhabit there; that the progeny of the first men might people that part also. . . To close this question with a sure lock, either the stories of such monsters are plain lies, or if there can be such, they are either not men, or if they are men, they are the progeny of Adam.[25]

In summary, Christian writers were prepared to accept a wide range of cultural and biological variation in that creature descended from Adam. Initial causes of man's diversity were accounted for in the sacred history of Genesis, but environmental causes were also accepted in explaining how variations continued to arise. Such diversity was thought to be coordinated with moral decline over the course of human history. In this view of our species, little attention was given to populations beyond their degree of relationship to the Christian fold, and diversity assumed a prejudicial aura. Only here and there do we glimpse a Christian scholar seeking to explain human variation outside the limitations of these guidelines of orthodox tradition. One such person was a writer of the sixth century who was sent to Spain to educate Visigoth

24. Herodotus's *History* was unknown in western Europe, save for limited portions, until 1474 when a Latin translation was prepared in Venice. More complete copies may have existed in Byzantium in the twelfth century.

25. McCraken, *De civitate dei.*

rulers in the fields of classical geography, zoology, and human anatomy. Isidore (560?-636), who was later archbishop of Seville, wrote a book entitled *Of Men and Monsters* wherein he accounted for cultural and biological differences in man on the basis of climatic changes affecting the seventy-three nations emerging from the progeny of Noah. He concluded that the monsters belonged within the human family after all, but as degenerate descendants of Adam's and Noah's lineage.[26] Isidore's successors were less interested in explanations of monsters than in elaborations of old and progressively more incredible tales about them.

SECULAR INTERPRETATIONS OF HUMAN ORIGINS

If one were to specify the single most important cause for the upsurge of interest in foreign peoples that marked the early Renaissance, it would be the exploration of new lands with their allurement of rich markets, rare products, slaves, and booty. Improvements in shipbuilding made it possible for the Portuguese to chart the west coast of Africa by the middle of the fifteenth century, and Christopher Columbus (1451-1506) reached the New World before the end of that century. In 1513 Vasco Nuñez de Balboa (1475?-1517) established that Columbus had found a new continent and not an eastern shore of Asia, the Indies, a fact substantiated by the circumnavigator Ferdinand Magellan (1480-1521). Asia was becoming better known with the development of trade routes into China and India.

Scribes were employed on exploratory expeditions for the purpose of writing reports of the geography, commercial products, and inhabitants of unfamiliar regions. Their accounts were read by scholars at home who compared their data with those of ancient and medieval travelers. At the same time, cabinets of curiosities, or Noah's arks, were being furnished with natural history specimens and man-made *curiosa* brought to Europe from distant places. This activity was coincident with a practice of collecting descriptions of foreign peoples into encyclopedias of ethnographic information. The most famous of these compilations include

FIGURE 2.3. Medieval monsters. From Rudolf Wittkower's "Marvels of the East: a Study in the History of Monsters." **Journal of the Warburg and Cortauld Institute** 5 (1942): 159-197.

Johann Boemus's (fl. 1520) *Omnium gentium mores, etc.*,[27] Sebastian Muenster's (1489-1552) *Cosmographiae universalis,*[28] and John Bulwer's (fl. 1650) *Anthropometamorphosis.*[29]

Some travel accounts were collected in a series and published as separate volumes, as

26. Wallace M. Lindsay, trans. *Isidori Hispolensis episcopi, Etymologarum sive libri XX, etc.* (Oxford: Clarenden, 1911), Book 11.

27. Edward Aston, trans. *The Manners, Laws, and Customs of All Nations, Collected Out of the Best Writers by Johannus Boemus Aubanus, a Dutchman, etc.* (London: Eld and Burton, 1611).

28. Sebastian Muenster, *Cosmographiae universalis* (Basle: H. Petri, 1554).

29. John Bulwer, *Anthropometamorphosis: Man Transform'd, etc.* (London: W. Hunt, 1653).

was done by Richard Hakluyt (1552-1616).[30] Other ethnographic writings were topical, such as Pedro Sarmiento de Gambóa's (1532-1608) *Historia de los Incas*[31] and Samuel Purchas's (1575-1626) *Purchas, His Pilgrimage,* which was a comprehensive study of religion.[32]

Unlike many of the medieval writers who were preoccupied with exotic tales of foreign peoples, scholars of the Renaissance were eager to obtain new and more accurate ethnographic data. Substantiation of fact from earlier accounts was no longer deemed necessary. They became interested in the physical appearances of hitherto unknown tribes, especially with respect to the variables of stature, complexion, eye color, hair form, and temperament. Descriptions of language, cultural institutions, ethical codes, laws, and the more mundane customs of house building and food preparation were included too. In 1587 Albert Meier (1528?-1603) wrote in German a guidebook for travellers that offered a list of topics to be investigated in a description of a foreign group.[33] Other handbooks were prepared in the seventeenth century that are the precursors of *Notes and Queries*, which anthropologists have found useful in the field for over a century.[34] Renaissance authors of ethnographic encyclopedias and handbooks were not indifferent to relevant sources of scriptural and ancient origin, and the recovered works by Greek authors were greatly respected. But the authority of earlier writings lost the hold they had enjoyed in the Middle Ages as seventeenth-century writers became more secular and theoretical in their approaches to all ethnographic data.

Coincident with this enthusiasm in acquiring and assessing information about foreigners, there arose questions not easily settled by reference to scripture or to the classics. How was the overwhelming diversity of human physical features, languages, and customs to be explained? What were the historical causes behind the settlement of the New World by a people not mentioned in the Bible or in ancient writings of the Greeks? Must all aspects of the phenomenon of human variation be accounted for within the brief 6000 years of sacred history?

Those who would uphold the church's stand on monogenesis favored the view that the Americas had been inhabited by immigrants from the Old World, arriving by sea from Europe or from northeastern Asia via the Bering Strait.[35] Perhaps the native Americans are the descendants of the Ten Lost Tribes of Israel. Or are they related to Greeks, Romans, Phoenicians, or even Scots and Welshmen?[36] Some monogeneticists held that they were survivors of the legendary continent of Atlantis, which was thought to have subsided into the ocean around 1320 B.C. The inhabitants of Atlantis were in the lineage of Noah.[37] Theories of this sort were founded upon the supposition that similarities of one or a few customs or words among American Indians and a group of ancient or contemporary people of the Old World provided proof of an historic connection. Account was not taken of the possibility that resemblances of customs and languages might be superficial, or due to independent de-

30. Richard Hakluyt, *The Principal Navigations, Voyages, Traffic and Discoveries of the English Nation* (London: George Bishop, Ralph Newberie, and Robert Barker, 1598-1600); George Bruner Parks, *Richard Hakluyt and the English Voyages* (New York: American Geographical Society, 1928).

31. Clements R. Markham, ed. and trans., *Narratives of the Voyages of Pedro Sarmiento de Gamboa to the Straits of Magellan* (London: the Hakluyt Society, 1895).

32. Samuel Purchas, *Purchas, His Pilgrimage, or Relations of the World and the Religions Observed in All Ages and Places Discovered* (London: William Stansby for Henri Fetherstone, 1613).

33. Albert Meier, *Certain Briefe and Special Instructions for Gentlemen, Merchants, Students, Souldiers, Mariners, etc. Employed in Services Abroad, etc.* (London: Iohn Woolfe, 1589). The English translation was published two years after the appearance of the original work in German.

34. *Notes and Queries on Anthropology*, 1st-6th eds. Royal Anthropological Institute of Great Britain and Ireland (London: Routledge and Kegan Paul, 1874-1951).

35. Edward Brerewood, *Enquiries Touching the Diversity of Languages and Religions through the Chiefe Parts of the World* (London: John Bill, 1614).

36. Robert Wauchope, *Lost Tribes and Sunken Continents: Myth and Method in the Study of American Indians* (Chicago: University of Chicago, 1962).

37. Ignatius Donnelly, *Atlantis: the Antediluvian World* (New York: Harper and Brothers, 1880); Lewis Spence, *Atlantis in America* (London: Ernest Benns, 1925).

velopment in different regions, or to coincidence, or to the diffusion of a custom or word. Migrations of tribes from an ancestral home in the Old World seemed to many the only possible answer to the enigma of the American Indians.

Human diversity could be accounted for within the framework of monogenesis by trotting out the venerable arguments for environmental determinism. Differences of climate and geography appeared to many thinkers to be the most important factors molding mankind into these many varieties. Tribes with customs, which were judged degenerate by Europeans, were relegated to the lower end of the human realm on the chain of being—the proper place for savages. More enlightened tribes were set in places closer to the locus of Europeans towards the upper end of the hierarchy. A famous writer of this concept of man's place in the chain of being was Michel de Montaigne (1533-1592) who, in an essay on cannibalism, attributed behavioral and temperamental characters of peoples to the features of their natural habitat. Environmental factors rather than innate psychic drives were causes of human variability, since the human mind assumed the stamp impressed upon it by the particular traditions of each social group. Biological variables were not correlated with customs in Montaigne's thesis.[38]

As early as 1512 the heresy of polygenesis was sufficiently threatening to the church to cause Pope Julius II (1443-1513) to proclaim that the American Indians were of Adam's seed and hence true men. This declaration did little to deliver native Americans from continuing exploitation by European adventurers, who considered them depraved savages, but it was an ecclesiastical attempt to counter the heresy that man had more than one center of origin and more than one set of original parents. However, the polygenesis hypothesis did no damage to the widely held and orthodox belief in the principle of plentitude in the model of the chain of being. Furthermore, to many writers the six millenia of sacred history was too short a period of time to account for the emergence of the great diversity mankind exhibits today in custom, language, and physique. Multiple creations seemed to be a more credible explanation for the variation of human populations. At the same time, this admitted more easily into the chain of being those quasi-human monstrous creatures who occupied the position between the manlike apes and savages. When chimpanzees and orangutans became known to European naturalists after 1625, the apes were as interesting for the philosophical issues their existence evoked concerning their place in the chain of being as they were with respect to their close anatomical and behavioral resemblances to man. Indeed, these considerations were inseparable. For a period of time there was confusion as to whether these creatures were enlightened brutes or simply degenerate men.[39]

Two proponents of polygenesis were the Swiss alchemist Paracelsus (1493-1541) and the French writer Isaac de La Peyrere (1594-1676). Both saw the account of Genesis to be descriptive of a special series of events affecting Adam's line, but unrelated to the origins and early lifeways of non-Jewish peoples. They interpreted the deluge to have been a local cataclysm in the Holy Land, not a universal event. In his writings of 1655, La Peyrere announced his *pre-Adamite* theory that Gentiles had an even longer history than the Hebrews, since the former had arisen from an earlier and quite distinct ancestor from Adam.[40] Other polygenecists published theories of multiple human origins, and their works served to bolster the arguments of apologists for the institution of slavery.

Arising from these attempts to explain human diversity and change within orthodox parameters of monogenetic degenerations, tribal migrations, and environmental determinism, or by the heretical thesis of polygenesis, a very different view of human history began taking form. Scholars have called this new approach to history the *doctrine of prog-*

38. Donald M. Frame, trans. *The Complete Essays of Montaigne* (Stanford: Stanford University, 1968), pp. 150-159.

39. John Greene, *The Death of Adam: Evolution and Its Impact on Western Thought* (Ames: Iowa State University, 1959), pp. 175-199 and C. D. O'Malley and H. W. Magoun, "Early Concepts of the Anthropomorpha," *Physis- Rivista di Storia della Scienza* 4(1962):39-63.

40. Isaac de La Peyrere, *Praeadamitae* (Amsterdam: 1655). ·

ress. It developed as a late Renaissance reaction to the assertion by theologians that man's Golden Age had occurred during Adam's period of residence in Eden, human affairs thereafter moving from bad to worse. Man's only hope of a return to a blissful existence lay in a life beyond the grave, and the waiting list was long and highly selective. The idea that man's greatest glory in this world lay in Greco-Roman antiquity seemed much more reasonable to secular classicists who came to be called *Humanists.*[41] In time they came to regard their own period of history as possessing advances in the arts and sciences that were unparalleled in antiquity. Furthermore, they recognized that some elements of ancient lore were faulty, as in the pre-Copernican model of the universe or Galen's (fl. second century A.D.) descriptions of human anatomy. History began to be interpreted as a process whereby civilization has moved, is moving, and will continue to move in a direction toward human betterment. Mankind, in all his varieties, is a perfectable creature whose goal is happiness in this present life on earth. Progress can be accelerated by the exercise of proper social laws that the philosopher may discover through knowledge and reason.[42] This secular concept of man's place in nature is in striking contrast to the medieval doctrine of human degeneracy and the teaching that happiness is to be found only in an otherworldly existence.

Expanded statements of the idea of progress appear in the eighteenth-century writings of Marie Jean de Condorcet (1743-1794)[43] and Anne Robert Jacques Turgot (1727-1791).[44] These scholars were influenced by Renaissance framers of the doctrine of progress, including Juane Luis Vives (1492-1540), who wrote an account of man's early history along the lines of Lucretius's earlier study,[45] and Francis Bacon (1561-1626), who championed experimental and inductive approaches to the study of natural science.[46] Another contributor to this philosophy was Thomas Hobbes (1588-1679).[47] Basic to their views of human history was the idea that customs, however different they may be from one population to another, all arise through learning and experience and not through supernatural intervention. Contemporary primitive peoples, be they considered noble or degenerate savages, were representatives of earlier stages of human history. As perfectable creatures, savages were worthy of ethnographic study in order that their more advanced and civilized brethren might document the earlier episodes of man's universal history. At the same time, savages were seen to be proper recipients of the blessings of civilization that were brought to them by missionaries and voyagers with economic motives. Pertinent to a study of human variation in space and time is the recognition by Renaissance philosophers that progress was the mechanism for change in custom. As the lifeway of a people improved, so their so-called *primitive* physical features underwent refinements, according to esthetic standards modifying them in the direction of more nearly resembling Europeans.[48] The idea of progress introduced time into the earlier notion that the lifeways of savages were unchanging, that these people had no true histories of their own in the European sense of that word.[49]

41. Humanism is an attitude about man's elevated place in nature. It was engendered through the study of antiquity and the classical heritage of grammar, history, poetry, rhetoric, and moral philosophy. Arising in Italy in the fourteenth century, Humanism spread rapidly throughout Europe, forming a background to the Reformation. The ideas of Humanism have persisted mainly in the curricula of schools. Writers identified as Humanists are Francesco Petrarch (1304-1374), Disiderius Erasmus (1466-1536), and Sir Thomas More (1478-1535).

42. John B. Bury, *The Idea of Progress: an Inquiry into its Origin and Growth* (New York: Macmillan, 1932).

43. June Barraclough, trans. *Sketch for a Historical Picture of the Progress of the Human Mind by Condorcet* (New York: Noonday, 1955).

44. Anne Robert Jacques Turgot, *Plan de Deux Discours sur l'Histoire Universelle* (Paris: Guillaumin, 1844).

45. Juane Luis Vives, *De causis corruptarum artium* (Antwerp: M. Hillenius, 1531).

46. Francis Bacon, *Novum Organum* (New York: P. F. Collier and Son, 1901).

47. Michael Oakeshott, ed. *Leviathan by Thomas Hobbes* (New York: P. F. Collier Books, 1967).

48. French social philosophers of the eighteenth century tended to be more optimistic over the potential advancement of savages exposed to the influences of civilization than were their colleagues in England and America.

49. Clarence J. Glacken, *Traces on the Rhodian Shore* (Los Angeles: University of California, 1967), pp. 3-33.

Believing that progress was a force operating intrinsically in all human societies, eighteenth-century philosophers sought to discover methods whereby mankind's early stages of development might be identified and described. Four approaches to this problem were developed: (1) the description of primitive societies, various tribes being regarded as representative of some universal stage of savagery or barbarism through which more advanced societies had passed during their course of development;[50] (2) the anatomical dissection and behavioral description of anthropoid apes carried out with the hope that these animals might be taught to speak or reveal in anatomical or mental characters some hint of man's primeval stage of social evolution;[51] (3) the observation of abandoned or feral children, such as the wild boy of Aveyron, Wild Peter of Hanover, and the feral child from Labrador, who were thought to possess minds untouched by the marks of civilization;[52] and (4) the exercise of inductive powers of reason, as Jean Jacques Rousseau (1712-1778) claimed could be productive of new insights when done by the enlightened intellectual. Rousseau favored the thesis, which was proposed earlier by other social philosophers, that a social contract bound primeval man to his course in civilized life.[53]

By the middle of the eighteenth century, educated Europeans agreed that a systematic approach to the accumulation of new data about human customs, languages, and physical characters held the answers to inquiries about man's state of nature, his different stages of cultural development, and the very essence of human nature itself. If universal customs and institutions could be sifted from studies with cross-cultural perspectives, it would be feasible for enlightened rulers more effectively to set their governments on the most direct course toward the goals of progress. At the same time, they would be able to administer their colonial enterprises more effectively. An interest in non-European populations led Western intellectuals to attempt an objective analysis of the history of their own cultural institutions. These precepts engendered a degree of cultural relativism and a desire to look at European culture without the limitations of a traditional ethnocentric bias. At this point

in history begins the scientific study of man. This is marked by its secular content, a desire to systematize ethnographic data, an historical orientation, and some conscious effort to free investigations from the weight of ancient authority and ethnocentrism. Empirical observation and comparative analysis, once put into practice, separate the early studies of human variation from those that have emerged during the past 200 years.

For Further Reading

Guthrie, William K. C. *In the Beginning: Some Greek Views of the Origins of Life and the Early State of Man.* Ithaca: Cornell University, 1957. This is a delightfully written study of Greek mythologies and philosophical speculations about the origins of living things, with special attention to man's primeval way of life.

Huddleston, Lee E. *Origins of the American Indians European Concepts, 1492-1729.* Austin: University of Texas, 1970. Various writings on the supposed historical connections of native Americans to peoples of the Old World are discussed.

Lovejoy, Arthur O. and Boas, George *Primitivism and Related Ideas in Antiquity: a Documentary History of Primitivism and Related Ideas.* Baltimore: Johns Hopkins, 1935. Here is a survey of the ancient roots of ideas relating to man's primeval condition, a topic that was of great importance to social philosophers of the eighteenth century.

Malefijt, Annemarie de Waal "Homo monstrosus," *Scientific American* 219(1968):112-

50. To Montesquieu, or Charles de Secondat, (1689-1755), the Persians best represented *natural man.* To Voltaire, or Francois Marie Arouet, (1694-1778) this place went to the Hurons of eastern North America. To Denis Diderot (1713-1784) the natives of Tahiti were the best examples of man in a state of nature.

51. James Burnett (Lord Monboddo), *Ancient Metaphysics: or the Science of Universals* (Edinburgh: J. Balfour, 1779-1795).

52. J. A. L. Singh and Robert M. Zingg, *Wolf-Children and Feral Man* (New York: Harper and Brothers, 1942).

53. Lester G. Crocker, ed. *The Social Contract and Discourse on the Origin of Inequality of Jean Jacques Rousseau* (New York: Washington Square, 1967).

118. Unusual illustrations accompany this discussion of ideas about halfmen and monstrous tribes of ancient and medieval fable. Belief in monstrous tribes was important to the concept of the chain of being.

Rowe, John H. "The Renaissance Foundations of Anthropology," *American Anthropologist* 67 (1965):1-20. The origins of comparative analysis in anthropology are attributed to the creation of a sense of perspective distance among Renaissance scholars of the classics. Ethnocentrism is eroded away by Western man's comparison of his own institutions with those of earlier times and with those of contemporary non-Western societies.

Shapiro, Harry L. "Anthropology and the Age of Discovery," in *Process and Pattern in Culture: Essays in Honor of Julian H. Steward.* ed. Robert H. Manners Chicago: Aldine, 1964, pp. 337-348. European reactions to newly discovered populations in Africa and the Americas are discussed, and the significance of early reporting of ethnographic data to the emergence of anthropology as a science is noted here as well.

Slotkin, James S., ed. *Readings in Early Anthropology.* Chicago: Aldine, 1965. This is a collection of original source materials that relate to anthropological topics. Statements about human origins, variability, and physical characters are among these writings from the fourteenth century to the close of the eighteenth century.

Bibliography

Bernheimer, Richard 1952. *Wild Men in the Middle Ages: a Study in Art, Sentiment and Demonology.* Cambridge: Harvard University.

Boas, George 1969. *The History of Ideas: an Introduction.* New York: Charles Scribner's Sons.

Taylor, Gordon Rattray 1963. *The Science of Life: a Picture History of Biology.* New York: McGraw-Hill.

3 | Development of the Race Concept

CLASSIFICATIONS OF MANKIND

Fundamental to the spirit of eighteenth-century science was the passion for classifying the phenomena of nature. With the introduction into Europe of unfamiliar varieties of plants and animals from newly discovered regions abroad, naturalists sought to bring order into their descriptions of these specimens. Unmethodically stocked cabinets of curiosity, long the place of amusement for the dilettante content to ponder grotesques of nature and human invention, were replaced by museums of natural history where carefully cataloged collections were maintained and studied. Naturalists had made considerable progress in structural studies of plant species more than a century before the Swedish botanist Carolus Linnaeus (1707-1778) published in 1735 the first edition of his work on the classification of living things, the *Systema naturae*.[1]

While not the first person to attempt to classify living things into discrete binomial categories, Linnaeus has been called the *father of taxonomy*.[2] The modern science of biological classification retains his system of arrangement of living things into hierarchies progressing from the most general to the most specific levels of organization.[3] In addition to this, Linnaeus developed a procedure for the formal description of organisms that was more efficient than the lengthy and detailed accounts of earlier investigators. In his youth, Linnaeus undertook a botanical collecting tour of Lapland. He completed his formal education in Holland, then spent the remainder of his life in the universities of Stockholm and Upsala. He attracted many students who collected plant and animal specimens throughout the world, and from their contributions he accumulated the data reported in the twelve editions of the *Systema naturae* that were published during his lifetime. It has been said that one-third of these dedicated young people perished on these collecting expeditions.

Like many naturalists of his day, Linnaeus was impressed by the fact that when plant seeds and shoots were grown in different environments, the mature forms had the capacity of developing quite distinctive features. When

1. Carolus Linnaeus, *Systema naturae in quo naturae regna tria, secundum classes, ordines, genera, species systematics proponutur* (Stockholm: G. Keisewetter, 1735).

2. The Swiss botanist Kaspar Bauhin (1560-1624) used a two-word system for identification and organization of plants. A *genus* name was followed by a *species* name, both rendered in Latin. For example, the English primrose is *Primula* (genus) *vulgaris* (species), while the cowslip is *Primula veris*. Bauhin's method foreshadowed the binomial nomenclature ascribed to Linnaeus, but the latter botanist applied it most effectively and consistently to animals as well as to plants.

3. Every organism in the Linnaean system has its place in a *class*, next in an *order*, a *genus*, and a *species*. The orders are the larger categories to which a number of genera with their species belong. Classes are still larger categories composed of several orders. Structural characters are the basis for the assignment of an organism to each of these categories. To this system, Linnaeus's successors added other categories, such as *phyla, suborders, families, subfamilies, superfamilies,* and so forth.

the same plants were cultivated in their original habitat, only one set of features appeared. It seemed that a transplanted specimen *reverted to type.* Linnaeus concluded that those variable characteristics that appear in plants of the same species must be due to the influences of climate and geography rather than to their hereditary properties alone. Regional manifestations of the same kind of plant were called *varieties,* a level of taxonomic organization below that of the species. While of interest, such subspecific forms are characterized by instability and were regarded as being of less taxonomic importance than specimens readily identifiable as good *types* of a species. Modern taxonomists define species as reproductively isolated populations related to one another. However, taxonomists of Linnaeus's time depended upon gross physical characters in their identifications of species. Controlled breeding experiments to establish species status are a feature of later experimental research, save among stock breeders whose interests in crossing domesticated animals were entirely economic.[4] To Linnaeus and to many of his colleagues and students, the determination of species was synonymous with isolating the essential characters of each kind of living thing placed on the earth by the Creator during the first week of the earth's history. Their conception of biological species was not new, for they were familiar with Aristotle's writings on animal kinds. But Aristotle had not worked out a classification of species or developed a methodology for the identification of familiar or unfamiliar species. In advancing the modern science of taxonomy, Linnaeus enjoyed referring to himself as the *Second Adam,* as he, too, was finding names for the beasts that share the earth with man.

Implicit in the eighteenth-century concept of species was the idea that the well-trained naturalist could discern from his examination of individual specimens the true *type* of the species, that idealized form that transcended all of the confusing varietal manifestations of a group of related organisms. Variation was a distraction to the classifier of nature eager to penetrate the essence of a species, particularly as the varieties themselves were sufficiently plastic to assume myriad expressions appropriate to different environmental settings. We recognize here the survival of the idea of nature present in the writings of Plato, where reality is ascribed to abstracted forms or ideal types and illusive properties characterize the individual expressions of every ideal form.

In the first edition of the *Systema naturae,* Linnaeus described his taxonomic methodology, used a binomial designation for genus and species, and assigned mankind to the animal kingdom along with the quadrupedal apes and sloths. These latter groups were called *Paradoxon.* In the second edition of 1740, the author divided the genus *Homo* into four geographical varieties identified by skin color. The category *Paradoxon* was dropped in the sixth edition published eight years later, and the genus *Homo* was defined by the ability of its members to comprehend such principles as the immortality of the soul, the soul's rational property, man's dominion over other animals, the perfection of the body as a wonderful machine, and the fragile and uncertain quality of human existence. As Linnaeus writes, "If you understand these things, you are man, and a genus distinct from all others."

In the tenth edition of 1758, Linnaeus includes two species within the genus *Homo.* Here we encounter for the first time the name *Primates* for the taxonomic order that includes the prosimians (lemurs, lorises, tarsiers), the monkeys of the New and Old Worlds, apes, and bats. The sloth disappears. Man is described on the basis of physical, cultural, and tempermental differences. Linnaeus presumed that these traits were the products of climatic and geographical determinants. His designation *Homo sapiens* may be rendered in English as *Man, the Reasoner.* The variety is indicated by the trinomial, as in *Homo sapiens*

---

4. Paleontologists (biologists who study fossil and other forms of preserved remains of extinct life) must establish taxonomic identifications upon anatomical criteria since other characters are usually absent in the specimens they study. They must determine if structural differences between fossil specimens reflect near or distant degrees of biological affinity. Characters that are expressions of a *normal range of variation* for a species must be distinguished from traits indicative of greater taxonomic distance. Linnaeus was not concerned with paleontological taxonomy, although he was aware of the existence and true nature of fossils.

americanus Linn. *Homo monstrosus* was the category of monstrous halfmen. Linnaeus included man among the Primates.

Linnaeus was the first naturalist to classify man in the animal kingdom and to use biological and behavioral traits as a basis for further subdivisions of the species into varieties. It would be unfair to ascribe racist motives to this effort, however. To be sure, Linnaeus held that his own culture was superior to others, but this is hardly an unusual point of view in the ethnocentric temper of his times. By attributing variation within any species to environmental influences rather than to inborn traits, Linnaeus drew upon the doctrine of progress with its conception of man as an improvable creature, providing that circumstances were present for his development in a

MAMMALIA

Order I.   Primates

Fore-teeth cutting; upper 4, parallel; teats 2 pectoral.

1. HOMO

sapiens
Diurnal; varying by education and situation
Four-footed, mute, hairy. ——— Wild Man **(Ferus)**

Copper-colored, chorleric, erect. —————————————————— American
Hair black, straight, thick; nostrils **(Americanus)**
wide, face harsh; beard scanty; obstinate, content free. Paints himself with fine red lines. Regulated by customs.

Fair, sanguine, brawny. —————————————————————— European
Hair yellow, brown, flowing; eyes blue; **(Europaeus)**
gentle, acute, inventive. Covered with cloth vestments. Governed by laws.

Sooty, melancholy, rigid. ———————————————————— Asiatic
Hair black; eyes dark; severe, haughty, **(Asiaticus)**
covetous, covered with loose garments. Governed by opinions.

Black, phlegmatic, relaxed. ————————————————— African
Hair black, frizzled; skin silky; nose **(Afer)**
flat; lips tumid; crafty, indolent, negligent. Anoints himself with grease. Governed by caprice.

monstrosus
Varying by climate or art.
Small, active, timid. ———————————————————————— Mountaineer **(Alpini)**

Large, indolent. ——————————————————————————— Patagonian **(Patagonici)**

Less fertile. ————————————————————————————— Hottentot **(Monorchides)**

Beardless. —————————————————————————————— American **(Imberbes)**

Head Conic. ————————————————————————————— Chinese **(Macrocephali)**

Head flattened. ———————————————————————————— Canadian **(Plagiocephali)**

2. SIMIA

FIGURE 3.1. Classification of man as given by Carolus Linnaeus. Based upon a translation of the Latin tenth edition of 1758 and a facsimile English edition of 1806.

salubrious habitat where proper nutrients for his body and Christian moral instruction for his soul were available. Linnaeus was willing to agree that varieties were unstable, but he was firm in his belief that higher taxonomic levels of species or genera were immutable and had remained so since the time of their creation. He could not conceive that new kinds of animals or plants could develop.[5]

The term *race* replaces Linnaeus's varietal subdivisions of *sapiens* in 1749 in the philosophical writings of the French naturalist Georges Louis Leclerc, Comte de Buffon, (1708-1788). Formerly *race* was a word reserved for breeds of domestic animals, but to Buffon it was applied to his sixfold classification of mankind. Each group was identified by biological traits of stature, skin color, and body form as well as by behavioral characters. Only Europeans escaped uncomplimentary descriptions. Buffon perceived the arbitrariness of all classifications and went so far as to reject Linnaeus's concept of species as an expression of the stable and idealized *type*. Just as varieties, or races, were mutable, so were species, according to Buffon. However, he agreed with his colleague that man belonged to a single species, our interfertility being the proof of our monogenetic origin.[6]

Buffon's belief in the impermanence of racial features led him to conclude that American Indians would have become more diversified in their pigmentation had they lived for a longer time in the New World. He entered into a heated debate with Thomas Jefferson (1743-1826) over his contention that native Americans had been physically and psychologically impaired by their existence in the humid climate of North America, an opinion that the distinguished Virginian regarded as insulting to all citizens of the new republic. Buffon went on to argue that Negroes had not yet had time to acquire fair pigmentation in the Western Hemisphere. There are degenerationist elements in Buffon's view of human variation for he thought that ancient men were stronger and taller, indeed were giants, but environmental factors operated to weaken all human races. Populations and even species that could not adapt to new environments were doomed to extinction.

Another classifier of mankind was the German anatomist from the University of Göttingen, Johann Friedrich Blumenbach (1752-1840). Like Buffon, he regarded the present-day races of man to be degenerative products of earlier pure racial types. In his book of 1776 concerning human origins and variation, Blumenbach writes that the agents of change are the environmental determinants of climate, food, mode of life, diseases, and degree of racial intermixture.[7] Not only did he accept the dogma of species immutability, but he maintained that once environmental determinants had cast their dye upon a population, the people would thereafter transfer their acquired traits to future generations by means of hereditary mechanisms as yet unknown. Man was not an exception to this rule that environmentally determined traits became hereditary characters distinguishing organisms below the level of species from one another. Human races were of the same order of taxonomic ranking as were to be found in varieties of a single species of animals under domestication.

But Blumenbach could not accept Linnaeus's placement of man among the beasts. Removing man from the Primates, he set him apart in an order of his own—the *Bimanes* or the two-handed creature. To the Linnaean varieties he added the Malay race, deleting

---

5. While maintaining that there are "as many species as issued in pairs from the hands of the Creator," Linnaeus later substituted genus for the species in this context, believing that "all the species of one genus constituted at first one species." He thought that new species might arise by intercrossing, since it was often difficult to distinguish some species from others. This tampering with the orthodox belief in species immutability caused Linnaeus to be censured by his colleagues.

6. Georges Louis Leclerc, Comte de Buffon, *Histoire naturelle, générale et particulière* (Paris: De l'Imprimerie Royale, 1749-1804).

7. Johann Friedrich Blumenbach, *De generis humani varietate* (Göttingen: Vandenhoeck, 1776); idem, *Abbildungen Naturhistorischer Gegenstände* (Göttingen: Dietrich, 1796-1810); R. T. Gore, trans. *A Manual of the Elements of Natural History by J. F. Blumenbach* (London: W. Simpkin and R. Marshall, 1825); Thomas Bendyshe, ed. and trans. *The Anthropological Treatises of Johann Friedrich Blumenbach* (London: Longman, Green, Longman, Roberts and Green, 1865).

from the earlier scheme the monsters and the feral men. He coined the term *Caucasian* to describe populations whose head form resembled that of a particular cranial specimen from the Georgian Caucassus, which was in his osteological collection. Along with this type specimen of European man, Blumenbach described four other skulls, each representing the idealized cranial form of the other geographical races of his classification.[8]

It is upon the taxonomic statements of Linnaeus, Buffon, and Blumenbach that later classifications of mankind have been based. Although some of their contemporaries voiced disapproval of any attempt to assign man to separate races, new classifications nevertheless emerged with great rapidity. Sorting criteria for racial taxonomies were variations of the sort already noted by the three pioneers, but cranial features became more important as time went on. The color of the skin was held to be very important, too, since it was regarded as a reliable indicator of other racial characters of which some, such as mentality, were not objectively assessable. Catalogs of human skulls were published of which the most famous in the nineteenth century were *Tabulae craniorum diversarum gentium*[9] and *Crania Britannica*.[10] The Philadelphia physician Samuel Morton (1799-1851) published *Crania Americana* in 1839, which was followed five years later by *Crania Aegyptica*.[11] In the previous century John Hunter (1728-1793) had an impressive collection of human skeletons in his museum in London that formed the basis for the present osteological series of the Royal College of Surgeons, London. Pieter Camper (1722-1789) assembled a craniological collection in Holland.

This enthusiasm over skulls was advanced by the popularity of the mystical notions of Franz Joseph Gall (1758-1828), the founder of the pseudo-science of phrenology.[12] The goal of phrenological procedures is to determine mental functions by the correlation of brain form with cranial shape. By attempting to relate mental functioning to anatomy, Gall satisfied many of his followers that a physical basis for intellect not only existed, but was also feasible to analyse along scientific lines. His work had important influences upon medicine, psychology, and early anthropology. Even

with the passing of the fad, osteological collections continued to be important to scientists' intent upon the study of man's biological variations and in the classification of individuals and groups into racial entities. Opinions as to the number of races there were in existence ranged from a conservative estimate of two, including some major subdivisions, to as many as several hundred!

There is no simple answer to the question of why an intense interest in human variation developed in the early part of the nineteenth century. The notion that man's biological traits were inherently linked to his behavioral traits became the essence of the race concept of this period, and this hypothesis had to be tested. The classifying of organic and inorganic phenomena was a primary goal of the natural sciences before and during this period, and it was inevitable that human populations should be arranged into groups according to their approximations to idealized types. Also varieties were essential elements of the concept of the chain of being, assuming the role of *missing links* between known species that were thought to be immutable. The instability of varieties, while a frustration to the taxonomist seeking to define the species *type*, had its place nevertheless, and *Homo sapiens* was not an exception to the thesis that all living things could be put into an hierarchical series. Man's range in the chain of being descended to the

8. This collection of great historic interest survives today at the University of Göttingen and has been described by the German anthropologist Laszlo von Karolyi in "Die Blumenbach-Sammlung in Göttingen (Ein Beitrag zur Geschichte der Anthropologie)," *Zeitschrift für Morphologie und Anthropologie* 57 (1966):192-198.

9. Gerardus Sandifort, *Tabulae craniorum diversarum gentium* (Leiden: printed for subscribers, 1830, 1838-1843).

10. Joseph Barnard Davis and John Thurman, *Crania Britannica* (London: printed for subscribers, 1856-1860).

11. Samuel George Morton, *Crania Americana* (Philadelphia: J. Penington, 1839); *Crania Aegyptica: or Observations on Egyptian Ethnography, Derived from Anatomy, History and Monuments* (Philadelphia: *Transactions of the American Philosophical Society*, 1844), vol. 9.

12. Franz Joseph Gall, *Sur les Foncions du Cerveau et sur Celles de Chacune de Ses Parties* (Paris: J. B. Ballière, 1825).

brute barely distinguishable from an ape and had at the opposite pole the most enlightened philosophers of the civilized world. Between these extremes were all the sorts and conditions of men that were manifested as varieties or races. Human variation was of interest, too, to Europeans and Americans standing on both sides of the slavery question. Apologists for slavery and other exploitive practices involving native peoples sought a scientific justification for their political dominance and colonial aspirations. Finally, classification and description of human populations provided an illusion that biological and cultural diversity had been explained according to scientific principles of unquestionable respectability. Of course the early nineteenth-century race concept did not explain anything for the reason that the isolation and identification of a varietal *type* was itself an abstraction and its sorting criteria arbitrary. But some writers of this period were keenly aware that racial classification per se could not shed light upon the broader problem of explaining how biological and cultural variations originated in the species. Their efforts to resolve this problem formed the theoretical basis for a study of man that is the hallmark of modern anthropological research.

MONOGENETIC THEORIES OF RACE FORMATION

Of that small group of scholars writing on questions concerning human variation between 1750 and 1850, the majority upheld the doctrine of the biological unity of man. They assumed that all species were immutable, and they were faithful to the philosophy that social progress was inevitable. Whatever primeval man might have been in visage and deportment, he was indubitably *Homo sapiens* and endowed with the capacity for improvement. Prehistoric skeletal remains had not yet been found in areas inhabited by early man, and it was generally held that our progenitors were not too unlike man today. Any explanations of our species' biological variations across geographical space today or in the past were to be sought in studies of contemporary populations. These ideas were held by men of whom some were followers of the teachings of Christianity while others were secular in their approach to scientific issues. None of

them were evolutionists. They looked to the phenomena of geographical habitat, climate, diet, and disease as playing a major role in the formation of human races, although differences of opinion existed concerning the specific effects of these environmental influences.

Among these writers of human diversity and race formation was the Reverend Samuel Stanhope Smith (1750-1819). He was a professor of moral philosophy at Princeton University and later president of that institution. He wrote that all human populations belonged to a single species, as demonstrated by man's interfertility today. But to this statement in support of monogenesis, he added that "the state of society which may augment or correct the influence of climate . . . is itself a separate and independent cause of many conspicuous distinctions among mankind." To this same essay, originally published in 1787, Smith added, "And in the continual migration of mankind, these effects may be still further modified by changes which have accidently taken place in a poor climate, and a prior state of society."[13]

Here is an early expression of two ideas held by later anthropologists: (1) cultural behavior plays a significant role in the biological constitution of a population and (2) learned habits may supercede in importance the effects of a single biological character induced by the physical environment. While not ascribing the origin of physical variations in man to culture, Smith was hypothesizing that certain biological traits initially brought into existence by environmental stresses could be altered through the influences of cultural innovations. For example, the black skins of Negroes could be attributed to the effects of tropical sunlight upon their unclothed bodies. However, the wearing of clothes could be conducive to the development of a lighter skin.[14] Believing that

13. Samuel Stanhope Smith, *An Essay on the Causes of the Variety of Complexion and Figure in the Human Species* (New Brunswick, N. J.: J. Simpson, 1810).

14. A black slave by the name of Henry Moss was examined by Smith. He considered Moss to be a case of a darkly pigmented person whose color was lightening. Smith thought this change was taking place because Moss wore clothes. Today we recognize that Smith was observing a piebald individual, one whose inheritance of a particular gene brings about a

all physical variables of our species are unstable under the influence of custom, Smith refused to accept the validity of any classification of mankind into arbitrarily conceived groups called races.

Another supporter of monogenesis during this period was the English physician James Cowles Prichard (1786-1848). In the five volumes of his *Researches into the Physical History of Man,* which appeared between 1836 and 1847, Prichard sought to explain human variation along the lines of scientific argument alone.[15] Unlike Smith, he did not look to scripture in support of his monogenism. However, he agreed with the Princeton professor that environment alone could not account for so many biological variables in our species because man's cultural behavior was *perpetually* exerting its influence upon physique. Then Prichard took himself several steps beyond Smith's premises by completely rejecting the idea that skin pigmentation was influenced by the environment. Nor could environment explain differences in man's variations of body size and form, shape of the head, and other physical characters. As to skin color, Prichard asked, how could sunlight be the simple cause when this trait continued unmodified over generational lines and in a great number of separate geographical regions? While Blumenbach would not have been dismayed by this question, Prichard wanted to penetrate the matter still further.

First he looked at single hereditary variations that appeared spontaneously at birth in certain individuals. Surely these must be the basis for characters that could become widespread in the populations to which these persons belonged. The new traits are preserved in subsequent matings that lead to the birth of viable offspring. Spontaneous variations are random in occurrence and not determined by environmental stresses. Older expressions for these phenomena were *sports* and *type deviants.* Today we describe these as *mutations,* their bearers as *mutants.*

Then Prichard noted that those species of plants and animals domesticated by man show a higher frequency of spontaneous variation than do wild forms of the same species. Like Blumenbach, he understood that variations within the human species are of the order of difference encountered in domesticated animals. From these observations, Prichard concluded that the racial forms of man are analogous to the breeds of dogs or cattle that man has reared by artificial selection under conditions of domestication. Prichard went on to observe that man is a self-domesticated creature. The varieties of mankind are produced by the effects of civilization, the major process in our own self-imposed domestication and our capacity for progress. He selected a single trait out of the many variable traits present in our species—the color of the skin. This he considered to be a good biological correlate of the degree of progress towards civilization attained by any human group. In short, the lighter the skin, the more cultivated the population being considered. Prichard decided that primeval man (including Adam and Eve) had skins that were black. Europeans of the present day are fair because of the beneficent influences of civilization, an attainment of earlier generations of darker skinned forebears. Darker skinned races today represented to Prichard gradations between the extremes of primeval black and contemporary civilized white.

While this correlation of skin color and level of social progress was attributed to the operation of a natural law, Prichard went on to argue that *sexual selection* was the mechanism whereby progressive changes in man's variability operated. He assumed that there was but one innate standard of beauty—light skin color—and individuals blessed with this trait would seek out mates of similar hue. In other words, white skins were most adaptive to civilized life, and sexual preferences guaran-

---

mottled appearance to the skin. This genetic defect occurs among all human populations, but is less obvious among sufferers whose skin color is already light. Moss, normal in every other respect, succeeded in buying his freedom from fees collected at the Black Horse Tavern in Philadelphia where he placed himself on display, demanding $1.25 per person as price of admission.

15. These volumes are preceded by Prichard's dissertation published in Latin: *Disputatio inaugural-is de generis humani varietate* (Edinburgh: Abernethy and Walker, 1808). There was a first English edition as well: *Researches into the Physical History of Man* (London: J. and A. Arch, 1813).

teed the continuation of this trend toward attainment or preservation of lightest skin colors in the more enlightened races. Dark skinned peoples persist only by a perverted aesthetic sense, according to this author.

Prichard is best remembered not for his contention that white races are superior to black races—hardly an unfamiliar idea in his day—but for his anticipation of Charles Darwin's (1809-1882) concept of natural selection. However, Prichard limited his theory of race formation to human groups alone, and specifically as an explanation for variations of skin color. Darwin, as we shall see, sought to explain the mechanism whereby organisms of *all* species were able to survive in the struggle for life.

Prichard's writings of 1813 exerted a strong influence upon the English anatomist William Lawrence (1783-1867), author of *Lectures on Physiology, Zoology and the Natural History of Man*.[16] Lawrence believed in the unity of mankind, in the fixity of species, and in the propriety of regarding breeds of domesticated animals as analagous to human races. Although he recognized the influence of climate, diet, disease, and custom upon the physical characters of populations, he questioned that acquired features could become inherited. Because environmentally induced effects terminate with the death of an individual, they could not be the sources of human variation transfered along generational lines. Instead, Lawrence argued, racial differences must be based upon the spontaneous appearance of variations.

Lawrence did not attempt to explain the causes for the sudden introduction of novel physical features, but he was confident that once an individual was born with a physical character distinguishing him from his parents and kin, his contribution might become preserved in his population. This was a natural phenomenon, and as an example Lawrence noted the abrupt appearance of a variety of short-legged, small-bodied sheep with crooked forelimbs, which had been bred in America from a single ewe that had given birth to a male possessing these unique characters. The offspring of this male had, in many instances, the same traits. The variety of sheep is known as *ancon*.

The search for examples of spontaneous variation in human populations now preoccupied Lawrence. He reasoned that when deviant individuals became reproductively or geographically isolated from their macropopulation they might become founders of new races. Such varieties were preserved by mechanisms analogous to those imposed by stock breeders upon their animals in attempting to select for propogation particular ones with traits deemed most desirable. In man, sexual selection operates towards the perpetuation of traits that are considered superior by standards of beauty in every culture. For an example, Lawrence turned to the idea that members of the European nobility possessed remarkable beauty of mind and body, features preserved in their lines because the selection of the most attractive mates was far easier for a prince than it was for a commoner! Under a hypothetical situation in which a royal lineage became completely isolated geographically, a new race might emerge in time.

Lawrence was not concerned with the problems of survival and adaptation in the struggle for life. Nor did he extend his theory of race formation in man into the broader sphere of all organisms in nature. Neither he, Smith, nor Prichard were evolutionists. Lawrence's idea of human race formation by spontaneous variation was criticized by his contemporaries on the grounds that human variation could not be explained by reducing causes to blind chance, a charge later to be leveled against Darwin and his supporters of the evolutionary concept of natural selection. But it would be difficult to argue that Lawrence had an original race theory, so profoundly was his work influenced by the ideas of Prichard, which he adopted and clarified. Both writers were innovative in their denial of the inheritance of acquired characteristics and in their thesis that new varieties might arise from spontaneous variations appearing in individuals and later becoming widely distributed in populations.

16. William Lawrence, *Lectures on Physiology, Zoology and the Natural History of Man* (Salem: Foote and Brown, 1828). On Prichard and Lawrence see Kentwood D. Wells, "Sir William Lawrence (1783-1867): a Study of Pre-Darwinian Ideas on Heredity and Variation," *Journal of the History of Biology* 4 (1971): 319-361.

Here was the real break with the traditional eighteenth-century notion of race formation.

Other writers of race theory sought to explain human variation in quite different ways. The French astronomer Pierre Louis Moreau de Maupertuis (1698-1759) had suggested that "an innumerable multitude of parts" resided in the reproductive fluids of animals, that these parts had the capacity to arrange themselves into configurations leading to the development of offspring similar to parents, and that random factors of some accidental penetrance of familial traits might result in novel assemblages and hence to new kinds of individuals.[17] Some of those offspring having new arrangements of parts would survive, reproduce themselves, and in time be the founders of new races. Because these new varieties were unstable, de Maupertuis argued, there was a tendency for aberrant individuals to become submerged within the macropopulation that would retain the norm of those traits identified with the type. While Prichard was to argue at a later time that black was the original skin color of mankind, the French astronomer thought the earliest men were white. Negroes were departures from this primal condition, but de Maupertuis could not explain why they failed to revert to the white trait. He conjectured that some selective mechanism must be operating to account for the fixity of certain physical types in the world. He decided upon sexual selection. Individuals who were not desirable as mates were forced to settle away from their parental populations, developing in isolation their unique traits until, having increased in numbers, they became recognizable as a separate race. The formulator of this hypothesis rejected the venerable notion of simple environmental determinism as the cause for variation in man, and his ideas have been compared to those of later evolutionary biologists who conceived of the mechanism of *genetic drift*.[18]

The Koenigsberg professor of philosophy, Immanuel Kant (1724-1804) also rejected the simple explanation of race as a product of environmental determinism.[19] He suggested that man's racial variations must be due to the emergence of particular latent powers that could be activated in individuals as essential adaptations under novel environmental pressures. Once expressed physically, these traits became a part of the hereditary constitution of a population. Thus, a capacity for the manifestation of *preadaptive* mechanisms was a special property of all living things. The environment could not induce new hereditary features to appear, but it could provide circumstances whereby they might arise. An organism's response to environmental variables was preordained. Kant classified man into four racial groups, using skin pigmentation as his most important criterion, explaining that this variable might be correlated to other markers of racial variation. He, too, was a supporter of monogenesis.

Finally we come to the ingenious ideas of race formation conceived by the Charleston-born physician Charles Wells (1757-1817).[20] During the American Revolution, Wells practiced medicine in London and wrote scientific papers on such topics as visual perception and the properties of dew. But he is best remembered for a paper entitled *An Account of a Female of the White Race of Mankind, Part of Whose Skin Resembles that of a Negro; with Some Observations on the Causes of the Differences in Color and Form Between the White and Negro Races of Man.*[21] This appeared in an appendix of a new edition of his other works, which were published in 1818, but the paper had been read five years earlier at a meeting of the Royal Society of London. Wells had seen a piebald woman, Hannah West, and from his observations formulated a

17. Pierre Louis Moreau de Maupertuis, *Venus physique, contenant deux dissertations l'une sur l'origine des hommes et des animaux; et l'autre sur l'origine des noirs* (Paris: Le Heye, 1745).

18. Bentley Glass, "Maupertuis and the Beginnings of Genetics," *Quarterly Review of Biology* 22 (1947): 196-210; Bentley Glass, Oswei Temkin, and William Straus, Jr., eds. *Forerunners of Darwin: 1745-1859* (Baltimore: Johns Hopkins, 1958).

19. Immanuel Kant, "Bestimmung des Begriffs einer Menschenrasse," *Berliner Monatsschrift* November 1785; idem, *Anthropologie in pragmatischer Einsicht abgefasst* (Koenigsberg: F. Nicolovius, 1798).

20. Kentwood D. Wells, "William Charles Wells and the Races of Man," *Isis* 64 (1973):215-225.

21. William Charles Wells, *Two Essays, One on Dew and the Other on Single Vision with Two Eyes* (Edinburgh: Archibald and Constable, 1818).

theory of race origins that is different from those we have just discussed.

Wells accepted the monogenesis doctrine and to it added that traits distinguishing major races from one another persist because they are correlated with innate defenses against disease. As a physician, Wells was well-aware that Europeans living in the tropics were vulnerable to maladies that did not have such deleterious affects upon native peoples, while tropical inhabitants frequently suffered and died of diseases to which men of the temperate zone had become adapted. While differences in skin color between the races of man were not the single cause of adaptive success in different environmental settings, it seemed reasonable to Wells that various physical traits, including the pigmentation of the skin, must have adaptive significance in guaranteeing survival of races within their native habitats. In other words, human races were formed as a consequence of different sorts of adaptations to climate and disease prevalent in various parts of the world. In any population, only those individuals would survive whose inherited traits assured that they would live to reproductive age. Less fortunate persons who were not endowed with the favorable hereditary constitution would succumb to death at an early age. With domesticated animals, new varieties had been observed to arise, and man could select from those strains that suited his ends. For man himself, spontaneous variations would be extinguished or perpetuated by a selective process inherent in nature. Wells believed that as man attained to higher levels of culture and so transcended his brutish origins, cultural institutions would reinforce the unique qualities of racial lines.

Some fifty years passed before Wells's paper on race formation received significant attention. When it was cited by Darwin in 1866 in the fourth edition of his *Origin of Species,* it was in the form of a brief acknowledgement that Wells had been the first person to recognize the principle of natural selection, although limiting the notion to a consideration of human races where its implications as a major evolutionary force of species formation were overlooked. Nor did Wells discuss physical characters other than skin color. Darwin was interested in the origins of all variable traits. However, the speculations of this obscure physician are of importance to us as an example of how natural scientists of the past century were moving away from the old theory of environmental determinism as the primary factor of human variability.[22]

POLYGENESIS

From this wide range of monogenetic theories, why had no single point of view gained general acceptance to the eventual exclusion of competing ideas? The writers we have been discussing were men of high intellectual attainments in medicine, natural history, or philosophy. They were proud of their powers of logical debate within the tradition of eighteenth-century veneration of reason over faith. To shake off the cloak of ancient arguments for environmental determinism, which had misled their predecessors, was their concerted goal. Yet their own theories of race formation became obsolete by the close of the nineteenth century, for some writers even within their own lifetime.

One major stumbling block to a universal acceptance of monogenesis was that its supporters were committed to explaining the emergence of all human races within the limited time scale of the Christian chronology. How could mankind have become so diversified within a mere six thousand years since the date of Creation?

Among the critics of monogenesis was Morton, the Philadelphian collector of skulls. While accepting the orthodox chronology as a fact that could not be contested, Morton observed that Egyptian tomb paintings dating to around 1500 B.C. depicted separate human races.[23]

How could such diversity have been accomplished within the ten centuries that had elapsed from the Creation to the date when the paintings were made? Surely a polygenetic theory of race formation was more reasonable

22. Richard Harrison Shryock, "The Strange Case of Wells' Theory of Natural Selection (1813): Some Comments on the Dissemination of Scientific Ideas," in *Studies and Essays in the History of Science and Learning Offered in Homage to George Sarton,* ed., M. F. Ashely Montagu (New York: Schuman, 1944).

23. Morton, *Crania Aegyptica.*

than any of the nc᷂ons contrived by Prichard, Lawrence, and their associates. Morton dated the miraculous adaptations of the human varieties to their respective geographical habitats to a time just subsequent to the biblical deluge. His ideas on polygenesis were very popular, and by the first half of the nineteenth century an *American school* of anthropology was respectfully recognized by Europeans as the product of Morton's genius. Before Morton's writings were read on the continent and in England, Henry Home, whose definition of race we have encountered already in the first chapter of this book, had published his essays in support of polygenesis.[24] He, like his American sympathizer, sought a compromise between Christian doctrines and a theory that could account for human variability within the limitations of the short time scale. Home regarded all men as descendants of Adam, but he set the time of their abrupt diversification into separate races to the period when the Tower of Babel was under construction. Not only did the Deity disrupt the original unity of men by imposing upon them a multiplicity of languages, but bestowed as well profound changes of biological and psychological patterns. Consequently, each group of people became, in an instant, miraculously adapted to different habitats over the face of the earth. Home was content that he had explained racial origins within the framework of Christian dogma.

Other polygenecists were equally confident, however, that their theories of human differences were more successful in averting the hurdle of the Mosaic chronology. Some opinions as to the degree of biological distance between human populations were extreme, even including the suggestion that Negroes were members of a separate species from the rest of mankind.[25] Josiah Clark Nott (1804-1873), a physician from Mobile, Alabama and an acquaintance of Morton's, declared that only the polygenesis argument could account for the inferiority of African peoples who had "risen but little above the beasts of the field." With George R. Gliddon (1809-1857), Nott published *Types of Mankind* in 1854, one of the most popular books on polygenesis. By 1871 it was going into its tenth edition.[26] While these writers turned to this theory as a scientific justification for slavery and maintained that the races of men were separately created species, their interpretations were not shared by all critics of monogenesis. Morton, for example, while having much to say about the inferior biological and mental status of the native peoples of Africa and the Americas, was nevertheless a firm abolitionist. The French writers on polygenesis, including Voltaire, proclaimed the natural right of all men to be free. They were less vocal in admitting that all men were culturally and biologically equal, however.

Supporters of both monogenesis and polygenesis conceived of human groups as types, be these classified into varieties, as Linnaeus had set forth in the *Systema naturae*, or as separate species. Classification of types was not the primary goal of the writers we have been considering here, and we have already noted that Smith rejected any effort to construct a taxonomy for man below the level of species. While some monogenists suggested that *new races* might be founded by individuals endowed with some spontaneous variation, they failed to appreciate the biological significance of normal ranges of variation of multiple traits present in populations. Their dilemma lay not in their inability to explain the causes whereby new characters arose in populations, for Darwin himself could not account for the mechanisms of genetic inheritance and mutation; rather they failed to realize that populations are open and changing genetic systems that do not crystalize as sharply defined racial types due to the sudden appearance of one or a few novel variations. Darwin's contribution to science was the demonstration that variable expressions of a biological character are significant in the broader context of a theory that applied not only to man but to all living things.

24. Henry Home (Lord Kames), *Sketches of the History of Man* (Edinburgh: W. Creech, 1774).

25. Robert Knox, *Races of Men: a Fragment* (Philadelphia: Lea and Blanchard, 1850). Knox (1791-1862) was an Edinburgh surgeon who lectured on the topic that successive generations of mulattoes became less and less fertile, a view without scientific standing today.

26. Josiah Clark Nott and George R. Gliddon, *Types of Mankind* (Philadelphia: J. B. Lippincott, 1854).

Before 1859 when Darwin published the *Origin of Species,* writers contributing to the emerging discipline of anthropology had already shifted from an eighteenth-century view of savages as perfectable but as yet unenlightened members of our own species, whose conditions of life were attributable to environmental factors, to a view that was less involved with the plasticity of mankind from forces outside his own nature. It was not a waning of enthusiasm about the doctrine of progress that characterizes this later period of the nineteenth century, but by 1850 more and more writers on human variation were ascribing differences between peoples to inborn, natural causes. There was now an effort to establish a population's true position along the road of human progress by discovering its innate qualities of mentality and physique. Racial determinism now came into competition with the idea of man as a psychically unified creature whose original innocence in a state of nature was altered by pressures from the physical and social environment.

To this change in interpretation of the affects of nature and nurture was appended the faith that racial differences could be explained scientifically, that a community of specialists—anthropologists—were able to resolve questions of racial variation with the same degree of confidence that had earned respectability already for scholars in other fields of natural science. At the same time that studies of racial variation were gaining scientific dignity, the non-Western peoples of the earth were being overwhelmed by new waves of European imperial expansion. Both economic and moral issues about slavery had reached a crescendo by the middle of the nineteenth century. So it was that the aspiration for a dispassionate and scientific study of human variation became trapped between the capitalist policies of colonialism and the ethical questions of human nature and freedom.

It is not difficult to recognize prejudicial attitudes towards nonwhite populations in the writings of Nott and Gliddon, men who upheld the American South's peculiar institution of commerce in human flesh. Biases we call racist today are present in the works of writers who abhorred slavery, some of them supporting

monogenesis while others rejected the theory. Many of the early anthropologists of the last century did not feel that their scientific study of human diversity was directly involved with political issues, but the very nature of their research material—mankind—meant that anthropological investigations were of interest to less objective writers. The questions about man that were raised by scholars endeavoring to

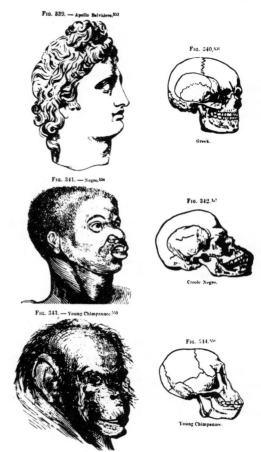

FIGURE 3.2. An illustration from a polygenecist text of 1854 wherein claims were made that the "lower races were connecting links in the animal kingdom and that the orangutan and chimpanzee are closer to people of African descent than these are to Teutonic or Palasgic types." From Josiah Nott and George Gliddon, **Types of Mankind.** Philadelphia: J. B. Lippincott, 1854, figs. 339-344.

work within a politically free area of inquiry dealt with the relative importance of the roles of nature and custom in the formation of races, the antiquity of certain variations, the ways new variations arose, and the stability of characters already present in a population. But before 1859 these questions were posed within the theoretical framework of monogenesis or polygenesis. It seemed to many persons of this period that the major task of anthropologists was to solve the problem of man's single or multiple origins.

DARWINIAN EVOLUTION

The Origin of Species by Means of Natural Selection, with its subtitle *The Preservation of Favored Races in the Struggle for Life,* is a book with two complementary theories. The first one is not original with Darwin, the idea that "each species had not been independently created" but had descended "from other species." Today we refer to the theory of descent of living things with modification as *evolution,* but in Darwin's day this was called the *transmutation* doctrine.[27] Where Darwin was original was in recognizing that this theory would not assume scientific acceptance until the mechanism by which this process operated in nature was identified. The second argument of the *Origin* concerns the nature of that mechanism which Darwin called *natural selection.*[28]

In the old-fashioned style of lengthy book titles, the principal themes of an author's work are summarized. Darwin followed this tradition, and if we examine closely the words he chose we can better understand the important points he wanted to make in enticing his readers into the pages of his book. Darwin was writing about *species,* not about higher taxa. He knew that if the origins of this basic unit of taxonomy could be explained, then a clear appreciation of the constitutions of genera, orders, and classes would emerge. He was not concerned here about the origin and antiquity of life. His title also reveals that he regarded a *selective* factor to be operating in the rise of new species from ancestral species. Furthermore this was a *natural* mechanism to be distinguished from the artificial selection practiced by breeders of domesticated animals and plants and from a supernatural interven-

tion of Providence. It is in the subtitle that we encounter a third important point. This is the claim that it is in *competition* for survival (i.e., in the struggle for life) that certain individuals will be favored by their possession of adaptive traits and so live to reproduce themselves: those individuals lacking these favorable adaptive features will die prematurely or leave behind them few progeny, thus reducing their contribution of traits to the succeeding generation.

In becoming aware that variations of individuals were, by virtue of their adaptiveness, critical to the biological success of a population living under ever-changing environmental settings, Darwin achieved a scientific revolution. He perceived something that had escaped the notice of taxonomic typologists: it was not the efficient design of a type specimen, but the variability of expression of biological and behavioral characters among individuals that insured the chances of survival for their populations. Furthermore, it was the slow accumulation of *minor* variations, not a sudden bound over the species line by the innovation of one or more spontaneous variations, by which descent with modification took place. Selection was operating at all times on organisms, Darwin wrote, even during the different stages of growth of an individual. Useful adaptations guaranteed survival. So it was that those varieties of the species, held in contempt as unsuitable objects of study by earlier biologists accepting the dogma of species immutability and venerating the notion of type specimens, were seen by Darwin to be the essential building blocks in the evolution of new species. The *Origin of Species* is as important for its presentation of an hypothesis accounting for the *how* of the evolutionary process as it is for its immense compilation of data

27. Another term once in common usage was *transformation. Evolution* was a term seldom employed by Darwin, but it became popular through the writings of the philosopher Herbert Spencer (1820-1903) beginning with a work he published in 1852. To Spencer the phrase "survival of the fittest" is attributed with reference to Darwin's concept of natural selection.

28. Charles Robert Darwin, *The Origin of Species by Means of Natural Selection, or the Preservation of Favored Races in the Struggle for Life* (London: John Murray, 1859).

documenting the fact of evolution. Darwin's work has been compared to the Copernican and Newtonian revolutions in the physical sciences and to the recent discoveries of the molecular basis for life itself. Evoked by the centennial in 1959 of the *Origin of Species's* publication, a number of exciting books and articles appeared on the subject of how Darwin arrived at the theory of organic evolution by means of natural selection.[29]

Some elements of Darwinian evolution, such as the effects of environmental stresses upon organisms and adaptive specializations of anatomy and behavior, had been appreciated since antiquity. Christian theologians were forever describing the phenomena of nature as God's handiwork, each creature being perfectly adapted to its place in the grand design. It was allowed that some modification of primal types was possible within the framework of environmental determinism. Spontaneous generation was admissible for insects, worms, and creatures holding a lowly place in the chain of being. There were some quasi-evolutionary speculations offered by two of the great scholar saints, Augustine of North Africa and Thomas Aquinas (1225?-1274) of Italy. They held that the Creator had endowed the earth with a life-giving potency to bring forth living things by a natural unfolding of a divine plan. The concept of the chain of being, while a static gradation of progressively more perfected inorganic substances, plants, animals, monstrous humanoid tribes, varieties of mankind, and supernatural beings, lacked only the qualities of time and change to become a rude model of evolutionary development. Already by the seventeenth century the chain of being was serving nonevolutionary taxonomists as their organizational framework. Finally, the doctrine of progress was developmental in its aspects of human perfectability, destiny, and admission of the possibility of social change. It was in the writings of Herbert Spencer that Darwinian evolution was woven into a philosophical thesis where social progress and biological evolution seemed inseparable components of a single process in nature.[30]

Anticipations of Darwinian evolution have been seen already in our discussion of Kant's ideas on the preadaptive properties of human populations, the concept of natural selection as it was proposed by Buffon and Wells, and the emphasis upon sexual selection in the racial theories of de Maupertuis, Prichard, and Lawrence. Another forerunner of Charles Darwin was his own grandfather, Erasmus Darwin (1731-1802). The younger Darwin was born seven years after Erasmus's death, but he knew of the latter's evolutionary interests through family stories and from reading the *Zoonomia, or the Laws of Organic Life* while in his late teens.[31] In this curious book, Erasmus Darwin wrote that all natural phenomena have an innate capacity for progressive transformations. Novel structures arise in response to new environmental challenges in the lives of organisms and, once acquired, pass on to future generations. Creatures unable to meet the stresses of their habitat were doomed to extinction, and Darwin pointed to the fossil record as evidence that many species of plants and animals had failed to survive into the present world. The elder Darwin applied his evolutionary theory to all of nature, not to certain elements, but his critics quite rightly noted that he had not explained the mechanism whereby transmutation of species could take place.[32]

More influential than Erasmus Darwin in disseminating the theory of organic evolution was Jean Baptist Pierre Antoine de Monet de Lamarck (1744-1829), a botanist who turned to the study of animals while associated with the Jardin du Roi in Paris.[33] His arguments

29. Loren Eisely, *Darwin's Century: Evolution and the Men Who Discovered It* (New York: Doubleday, 1958) and Gertrude Himmelfarb, *Darwin and the Darwinian Revolution* (London: Chatto and Windus, 1959).

30. For a discussion of pre-Darwinian evolutionary theory see Henry Fairfield Osborn, *From the Greeks to Darwin: an Outline of the Development of the Evolution Idea* (New York: Macmillan, 1894).

31. Erasmus Darwin, *Zoonomia, or the Laws of Organic Life* (New York: T. and J. Swords, 1794-1796).

32. Desmond King-Hele, *Erasmus Darwin* (New York: Charles Scribner's Sons, 1963).

33. Today this is called the Jardin des Plants. This park is worth visiting to see its collections of plants and animals preserved since Lamarck's day in some of the buildings where he carried out his research. Here you will find even today a flavor of early nineteenth-century natural history museums.

begin with the premise that because environments undergo change over time, so must their inhabitants if the latter are to survive. Adaptation is possible because organs have the capacity to develop to a degree that is proportional to their usefulness. Unlike Buffon and Blumenbach who saw variations reflecting the degenerative departures of organisms from an early purer form, Lamarck considered that variations developed as necessary responses to new challenges organisms faced in their habitats. He went on to explain that there were *felt needs* expressed by an animal that could be engendered in its offspring by the structural refinement of an organ or by the sudden appearance of a new structure necessary for its survival. To this French naturalist, this process whereby living things acquired new and better adaptive structures must be a progressive one, both in the historical sense that highly complex animals and plants become transformed over long periods of time from simpler ancestral organisms, but also for the reason that its effects are continuous. By putting time and mobility into the chain of being, Lamarck altered the static model of life into a dynamic one with continuity between species. The fossil record documented the fact that organisms had become modified over time, ancient species giving rise to new species ad infinitum. Concerning human variation, Lamarck observed in his famous work of 1809, *Philosophie zoologiques,* that there were six races, the most recent products of the transmutation process. Mankind arose from ancient apes who had acquired language by the formation of speech organs in response to their felt needs for communication![34]

Before turning to the story of Charles Darwin and the concept of natural selection, we should note that amazing book published anonymously in 1844—*Vestiges of the Natural History of Creation.*[35] Falsely attributed to Prince Albert, the Countess Lovelace (Lord Byron's daughter) and to several other notables of the period, it was revealed eventually to be the effort of the distinguished publisher of encyclopedias and books on travel, Robert Chambers (1802-1871) of Edinburgh. Although a staunch supporter of the transmutation hypothesis, Chambers put together such a disreputable hodgepodge of scientific and mystical interpretations of the subject that he earned the contempt of many naturalists who were sympathetic to the idea of evolution. Charles Darwin held the *Vestiges* in low esteem, but grudgingly confessed that the furor it created in scientific circles helped to disperse some of the fire he was certain to draw with the publication of his own carefully documented work of 1859. *Vestiges* brought to the forefront of public knowledge that there were more than a few writers on the topic of transmutation theory, that Lamarck had not said the last word on the matter. All readers of Chambers's book could see that he was no more successful than Lamarck or Erasmus Darwin in accounting for the mechanism controlling the process of descent with modification. Thus the field of inquiry lay open to Charles Darwin.[36]

If you allow yourself the pleasure of an evening's reading of Darwin's delightful autobiography, you may be startled by its author's admission that his forerunners, writing on evolution and race formation in man, played an insignificant role in the series of conceptual steps leading to his discovery of natural selection.[37] Indeed, Darwin learned about Wells from his friends, and in successive editions of the *Origin of Species* new names of persons who had conjured with the problem of evolution are dutifully cited. Even Lamarck's works he knew at secondhand, initially from an acquaintance at Edinburgh, Robert E. Grant (1793-1874), and later in the writings of the Scottish geologist Charles Lyell (1797-

34. Hugh Elliot, trans. *Zoological Philosophy: an Exposition with Regard to the Natural History of Animals by Jean Baptiste Pierre Antoine de Monet de Lamarck* (London: Macmillan, 1914).

35. Anonymous (Robert Chambers), *Vestiges of the Natural History of Creation* (London: J. Churchill, 1844). See Milton Millhauser, *Just Before Darwin: Robert Chambers and 'Vestiges'* (Middleton: Wesleyan, 1959).

36. Historians of science have cited other forerunners of Darwin, but space does not allow for their discussion here. The interested student should see the writings of Etienne Geoffroy St. Hilaire (1772-1844), Edward Blyth (1810-1873), and Patrick Matthew (1790-1874).

37. Nora Barlow, ed. *The Autobiography of Charles Darwin, 1809-1882* (New York: W. W. Norton, 1969).

1875). We have noted already that Darwin was unmoved by his reading of the *Zoonomia,* and his impression of his grandfather's work was not improved upon reading the book again after his five-year voyage around the world on the H.M.S. *Beagle.* It is to the experiences of this travel venture that Darwin attributed the awakening of an interest in natural history that transcended the casual involvement in biology and geology he had enjoyed as a youth. When Darwin boarded the *Beagle* at the age of twenty-two, he had experienced an unsuccessful and aborted course of medical studies at Edinburgh followed by an undistinguished academic record at Cambridge, which he attended with vague plans for eventually becoming a country parson. Charles's father, Robert Darwin (1766-1848), had abandoned hope in his son's future, once denouncing him as good only for a sportman's life of shooting and cross-country hedgehopping.

During the long years of his tenure as naturalist of the circumglobal expedition of the *Beagle,* the young Darwin became converted to the theory of evolution. This was not a simple and straightforward intellectual metamorphosis but a change of mind that was gradual, sometimes painful, and always frustrating. Upon reading Lyell's *Principles of Geology,* of which the first volume was published in 1830 and given to him for shipboard reading by his botany professor at Cambridge, John Stevens Henslow (1796-1861), Darwin came to see that the antiquity of the earth and its inhabitants must be far greater than the age offered by the Mosaic chronology.[38] Perhaps the earth was of even greater antiquity than accorded it by certain geologists of the day who explained our planet's history by a theory that geomorphological features were products of successive watery episodes, of which Noah's flood was the latest manifestation.[39] Lyell's approach, called *uniformitarian geology,* was based upon the studies of his Scottish compatriot James Hutton (1726-1797). The latter held the view that the earth's central heat and pressures built up by this heat have been most important in the shaping of the terrestrial surface of the globe. But the uniformitarian geologists went beyond the matter of geomorphological agents to the question of the age of the

earth itself. They were unconcerned with correlating geological events with scripture, and their suggestion that the earth's antiquity was of unfathomable degree was a call to arms of those geologists seeking to preserve some vestige of the account rendered in Genesis.

At the time Darwin was deep into his study of Lyell's uniformitarianism, a rival geological doctrine was being advocated in France by the paleontologist Georges Cuvier (1769-1832). While accepting the role of both water and fire in the formation of the earth. Cuvier proposed that a series of cataclysmic episodes had taken place. This could be demonstrated, he said, by the deposition of different species of fossilized remains from stratified beds in the region of the Paris Basin.[40] Cuvier's catastrophic geology is not unlike the theory of Hutton and Lyell insofar as it grants a great age to the earth, but the theses are irreconcilable on the question of process. To the Scottish geologists there was no evidence to indicate a succession of worldwide catastrophes bringing about extinctions of living things, save for a few survivors left over to populate the next world. Rather, the uniformitarians proposed that catastrophic upheavels are limited to local events and have been of relatively minor degree. All geological formations are explicable on the basis of familiar natural processes operating in the world today. Gradual changes repeated over seemingly limitless spans of time could account for all features of past and present terrains, according to these opponents of Neptunism and Cuverian catastrophism.

Darwin was impressed by what he read in the *Principles of Geology,* for if the earth told a story of gradual changes of landscape over

38. Charles Lyell, *Principles of Geology* (London: John Murray, 1830-1833).

39. *Neptunist geology* is associated with the German minerologist Abraham Gottlob Werner (1750-1817) of Freiberg and his Scottish disciple Robert Jameson (1774-1854) of Edinburgh. Charles Darwin attended Jameson's lectures at Edinburgh, recalling them as very dull.

40. Henry M'Murtrie, ed. and trans. *The Animal Kingdom Arranged in Conformity with its Organization, by Georges Cuvier* (New York: Carvil, 1831) and Robert Jameson, ed. *Essays on the Theory of the Earth by Georges Cuvier* (Edinburgh: W. Blackwood, 1818).

long periods of time, then might not its inhabitants have had a continuous biological history? Cuvier had shown by his paleontological investigations that ancient creatures were often quite different from living species, some earlier species even having become extinct and without direct survivors, but he had misinterpreted the presence of different kinds of fossils in separate strata to mean that there had been episodic stages of biological change. Darwin, while accepting the fact of species extinction from his own observations of fossils scattered across the plains of Argentina, noted that some of these ancient forms, in particular the armadillolike creatures, were not too unlike living species. This suggested to him that the extinct forms might be ancestrally related to living armadillos, the physical variations distinguishing the early and present-day forms from one another being the products of slow, adaptive modifications over time. Here was biological variation observed in uniformitarian and temporal perspective.

The young naturalist turned to spatial dimensions of variation when he noted that there was a geographical replacement of allied kinds of animals and plants over the regions he traversed in collecting his specimens. He was interested in the populations of large flightless birds that occupied adjacent regions. Yet these creatures belonged to two separate species. In areas adjoining their habitats lived different but related varieties of both species. Such observations led Darwin to speculate that apparently minor variations of a structure might have adaptive significance for organisms of a single species over its geographical range. This fact was most forcefully brought home to him when the *Beagle* harbored at the Galapagos Islands, a cluster of volcanic bits of land rising from the ocean floor some 650 miles off the coast of Ecuador. Uninhabited until the sixteenth century, these islands possessed an essentially South American fauna rather than one characteristic of the Pacific area. Yet species of land and sea iguanas, tortoises, finches, and other creatures survive here and are distinct from mainland species. Darwin recognized that the isolation of these animals was a crucial part of the question of their uniqueness. Even on the separate islands the varieties were different. The earliest reptiles, amphibians, and birds that had settled on the islands from the mainland must have been chance migrants of species present in greater numbers there, but isolation in these different environmental settings over the course of generations had led to a situation whereby new varieties had developed. As these varieties became more specialized in their structural and behavioral adaptations to particular ecological niches on the islands, they became reproductively isolated from each other and so gave rise to new species. Geographical isolation could be seen as one condition for the origin of a new species from ancestral forms assignable to different albeit related species.

By the time Darwin returned to England in 1836 he was well known to naturalists there as his collections had been shipped home from abroad and preceded him. Completely converted to uniformitarian geology and to the theory of organic evolution, Darwin now set about searching for the mechanism by which the process of modification of living things came about. He read extensively during this time, talked to stock breeders and gardeners to learn more about the results of their experiments in artificial selection, discussed his interests with Lyell, Henslow, and a coterie of friends, then began an eight-year study of variations in a single animal group, the barnacles. The catalyst, whose reaction with the travel experiences and observations brought forth the concept of natural selection, was Darwin's reading in 1838 of an essay by the English clergyman, Thomas Malthus (1766-1834). Then for the next twenty years Darwin collected data from his notebooks and the scientific literature to substantiate his thesis that he had discovered the means by which the evolutionary process took place. We know that Darwin was working on his hypothesis during these early years because of the *sketches* he wrote for himself in 1837, 1842, and 1844.

Malthus was not an evolutionist or, for that matter, a champion of the doctrine of progress. When he wrote his *Essay on the Principles of Population* in 1798, he was attacking both those social philosophers who had forecast man's future as bright and upwardly progressive as well as the technocrats of his day who had faith in the benefits of unrestricted urban growth during the early phases of the Industrial Revolution in England. Malthus noted that populations increase geometrically while food resources increase arithmetically. This sets up a competitive dynamic whereby population growth is checked only by the failure of some individual organisms to obtain the food necessary for their survival. Among animals this control is expressed by "waste of seed, sickness, and premature death," while man perishes from "famine, disease, war and vice." The good parson described this process as remorseless and inevitable so long as man did not control his numbers. Hence those efforts of the believers in progress and industrialization to assist their fellowman by increasing prosperity, happiness, and circumstances condusive for procreation were hastening the day of ultimate doom of all mankind.[41] Darwin, a firm believer in progress, took from Malthus's essay the element of competition in nature, the *struggle for life*. Given the fact that organisms exhibit variations, that some characters are more adaptive than others, and the element of competition that favors the survival of organisms with the most favorable traits, Darwin conceived of the means by which evolution worked. This process is natural selection. New species could rise from those organisms possessing favorable variations, while creatures lacking these characters died or left fewer progeny. The fossil record is the graveyard of many extinct species, although some ancient lines are directly ancestral to living species.

Another reader of Malthus's essay was the English naturalist Alfred Russell Wallace (1823-1913). He was also familiar with Darwin's narrative of the voyage of the *Beagle*, Lyell's geological works, and Chambers' *Vestiges*. Interestingly enough, Wallace was converted to evolutionary theory after reading Chambers's famous book. He had carried out researches in Brazil and on the Malay Archipelago, and his reputation as a biologist was well established. What brings Wallace into our story is that he wrote a letter to Darwin in 1858; it revealed that he had independently conceived of natural selection as playing a role in evolution. With the magnanimity typical of Darwin, Wallace was asked to put together a paper summarizing his views. This, with Darwin's report, was read at a meeting of the Linnean Society of London on the evening of July 1, 1858. The *Origin of Species* was published the following year, Wallace making additional contributions to their thesis soon thereafter.[42]

Critics of the *Origin of Species* were many and vocal, refusals to accept Darwin's theory being based upon various points. There was the matter of accepting the reality of organic evolution itself, but even for those who favored the concept the question remained if Darwin had truly discovered how evolution operated. The fossil record was frustratingly incomplete and did not satisfy the demands of some critics that missing links be identified between extinct and contemporary species. As to creatures sharing the earth with man, had a case of one species evolving into another ever been observed? Theologians were defensive about their arguments for beneficient design in nature, not to mention their fear of a heresy that conferred upon nature rather than upon her Creator a self-sufficiency to regulate her domain. Darwin scrupulously avoided any mention of man in 1859, beyond suggesting at the end of the book that by the study of evolution "light will be thrown on the origin of man and his history."[43] Much of the dissent over the *Origin of Species* centered upon the issue of how variable expressions of a character came into existence. Darwin had dealt with the matter of the fate of variable traits, but he and his colleagues could not account for the origin of variations. Some rather interesting ideas were proposed on this issue, but the notion of the inheritance of acquired characters still held an important place. Real progress was not made in this area of research until after 1900, although the foundations of the modern science

41. Thomas Malthus, *An Essay on the Principle of Population* (London: J. Johnson, 1798).

42. Alfred Russell Wallace, *Contributions to the Theory of Natural Selection* (New York: Macmillan, 1870) and idem, *Darwinism* (New York: Macmillan, 1889).

43. For modern views on the relationship of Christian doctrine and contemporary evolutionary theory see C. J. Wideman and R. Gehlen, *The Biological World* (Chicago: Loyola University, 1962), pp. 474-481 and Declan Sheedy, "A Catholic View of Evolution," *United States Catholic,* (August 1964), pp. 10-12.

of genetics were being laid down in the 1860s by a Moravian monk Gregor Mendel (1822-1884), who experimented with the hereditary properties of garden plants. Ironically the successes of this little-known investigator escaped the notice of Darwin and his colleagues.

Another problem relating to variation had to do with the question of how evolution could take place given the slow rate of accumulation of slight variations in the formation of new species. Even granting a profound antiquity to the earth and living things, how could such a tedious process account for the existence of so many different kinds of life in all their varietal expressions? Every organ was the target of natural selection or had, at least, been necessary for survival at some period in the evolutionary history of a population. Vestigial organs, such as gill slits in the embryos of mammals and the coccygeal vertebrae in man, might be

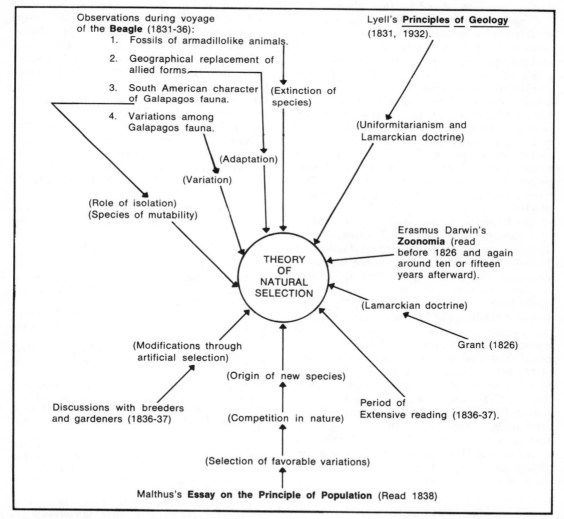

FIGURE 3.3. Schematic representation of the major lines of speculation which led Charles Darwin to the concept of natural selection. Based upon Darwin's own reconstruction of his ideas as reported in his **Autobiography.**

evidence of descent from ancestral forms where such structures were adaptive, but even their earliest manifestations must have arisen from a gradual development of minor variations. These matters of time and change troubled Darwin and led him to consider processes that might be complementary to natural selection whereby rates of evolutionary change could be accelerated. His interest in sexual selection, described in his book of 1871, *The Descent of Man and Selection in Relation to Sex*, was engendered by this dilemma.[44]

Despite these issues of debate, the number of Darwin's supporters grew, first among his immediate British associates in the biological and geological sciences, then among embryologists of whom the German Ernst Haeckel (1834-1919) was fanatically loyal. Haeckel sought evidence of the evolutionary process in the prenatal development of animals.[45] French biologists were slow to admit their debt to Darwin, claiming Lamarck as the true exponent of evolution. Cuverian geology retained some influence in that country, hence uniformitarian attitudes, so evident in Darwinian gradualism of biotic change, were also greeted with suspicion on the other other side of the Channel. Among American naturalists Darwin's chief defender was Asa Gray (1810-1888), a professor of zoology at Harvard.[46] But of all Darwin's apostles, no one furthered his cause with higher spirits than the young English biologist, Thomas Henry Huxley (1825-1895), "Darwin's bulldog." He faced squarely the issues of how man was a product of evolution as demonstrated by comparative anatomy of apes and man.[47] We have already noted the enthusiasm of Spencer for the theory of organic evolution in compiling data to support his philosophy of social progress. Upon reading of Darwin's concept of natural selection in 1859, he immediately applied it to his view of life, emphasizing that natural selection operated in the political and economic world of man.[48] Meanwhile, Wallace was applying the concept of natural selection to the study of racial variation in man.[49]

RACIAL ANTHROPOLOGY

The effects of Darwinian evolution upon race theory were not immediately apparent following the publication of the *Origin of Species,* but by the end of the nineteenth century the cumulative aspects of an evolutionary approach to the study of human variation had become obvious.[50] The early anthropological societies emerged from older established scientific organizations wherein the study of human variation was of peripheral interest: the Royal Society of London founded in 1660, the Musée d'Histoire Naturelle of Paris founded in 1789, the Linnaean Society of Boston founded in 1814, and so forth. Among the first societies of anthropology may be included the Société d'Anthropologie founded in Paris in 1858 by the anatomist Paul Broca (1824-1888), the Ethnological Society of London established in 1843, and the parent of the Anthropological Society of London born some twenty years later. From 1865 to 1871 anthropological societies were begun in Moscow, Berlin, Vienna, Stockholm, and Florence. The American Ethnological Society was meeting in New York by 1842. These organizations and a number of successors published periodical journals and research reports, held conferences, established

44. Charles Robert Darwin, *The Descent of Man and Selection in Relation to Sex* (London: John Murray, 1871).

45. Ernst Haeckel, *The History of Creation: or the Development of the Earth and Its Inhabitants by Action of Natural Causes. A Popular Exposition of the Doctrine of Evolution in General and that of Darwin, Goethe, Lamarck in Particular,* trans. E. Ray Lankester (New York: D. Appleton, 1876).

46. A. Hunter Dupree, *Darwiniana: Essays and Reviews Pertaining to Darwinism by Asa Gray* (Cambridge: Harvard University, 1860).

47. Thomas Henry Huxley, *Evidence as to Man's Place in Nature* (London: Williams and Norgate, 1863).

48. Herbert Spencer, "A Theory of Population Deduced from the General Law of Animal Fertility," *Westminster Review* 57 (1852):468-501 and idem, *The Principles of Biology* (New York: D. Appleton, 1864-1867).

49. Alfred Russell Wallace, "The Limits of Natural Selection as Applied to Man," in *Natural Selection and Tropical Nature: Essays on Descriptive and Theoretical Biology,* ed. Alfred Russell Wallace (London: Macmillan, 1870).

50. T. Dale Stewart, "The Effects of Darwin's Theory of Evolution on Physical Anthropology," in *Evolution and Anthropology: a Centennial Appraisal*; ed. B. J. Meggers (Washington, D.C.: The Anthropological Society of Washington, 1959), pp. 11-25.

libraries and museums, and maintained tangential contacts with craniological and ethnological collections housed by various institutions. The Czechoslovakian-born American anthropologist Ales Hrdlicka (1869-1943) gave 1866 as the date for the attainment of a mature level of academic work in biological anthropology in the United States, a year marked by the founding of the Army Medical Museum in Washington, D.C. and the Peabody Museum in Boston. Anthropological studies entered the university curriculum by the middle of the nineteenth century with the occupation of academic chairs by persons engaged in anthropological research. The first professor of anthropology was Armand de Quatrefages (1810-1892) of Paris who assumed this position in 1856. Higher degrees for students of the discipline were granted before the turn of the century, the first two Doctor of Philosophy degrees in anthropology being conferred in the year 1892 at the University of Munich and Clark University in Massachusetts.

The rapid development of anthropology has been described elsewhere in greater detail, but mention of a few major developments will put in perspective the kinds of questions about human variations that were being asked between 1859 and 1900.[51] The science of genetics came into existence in the twentieth century, but new techniques had been invented prior to that time for measurement and morphological description of variable traits found in human populations. Osteological collections were growing in size and number at research institutions that were staffed with anthropologists carrying out research on human variability.[52] The methodology of accurate measurements and morphological observations of the human body is called *anthropometry,* and by 1900 the development of special instruments for this purpose had come a long way from the earlier techniques of the phrenologists.[53] The application of anthropometric procedures had shifted from quantitative descriptions of ape and human differences to measurements of human variations. Broca introduced statistical methods into the study of skeletal series, claiming that at least twenty skulls must be in a series for accurate determination of racial affinity. His interests in brain anatomy ini-

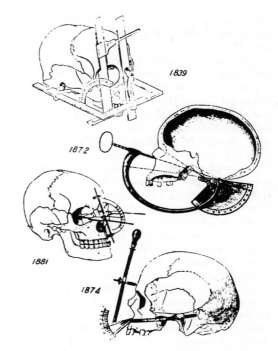

FIGURE 3.4. Early anthropometric instruments. 1839—Morton's facial goniometer; 1872—Broca's occipital goniometer; 1874—Broca's median facial goniometer; 1881—Atkinson's facial goniometer. From Lucile E. St. Hoyme, "Physical Anthropology and its Instruments," **Southwestern Journal of Anthropology** 9 (1953): 416, fig. 3.

tiated the study of soft part analysis of living subjects. The soft part anatomy has to do with the study of nonosteological tissue, such as

51. Marvin Harris, *The Rise of Anthropological Theory: a History of Theories of Culture* (New York: Thomas Y. Crowell, 1968) and Annemarie de Waal Malefijt, *Images of Man: a History of Anthropological Thought* (New York: Alfred A. Knopf, 1974).

52. For a description of osteological collections in the United States see Alés Hrdlička, "Physical Anthropology in America," *American Anthropologist* 16 (1914):508-554 and "Physical Anthropology: its Scope and Aims: its History and Present Status in America," *American Journal of Physical Anthropology* 1 (1918):3-23, 113-182, 267-304, 377-414.

53. Lucile E. St. Hoyme, "Physical Anthropology and its Instruments: an Historical Study," *Southwestern Journal of Anthropology* 9 (1953):408-430.

skin, cartilage, and muscle. One observation taken on skulls and the living head is the *cephalic* (or *cranial*) *index*. This is the ratio of the measurements of the maximum length and breadth of the cranial vault. It was conceived by the Swedish anthropologist Andres Retzius (1796-1860). Long and narrow heads are *dolichocephalic;* short and broad heads *brachycephalic*. Descriptions of cranial form were thought to correlate well with other variations. A method for determining the internal capacity of the skull was invented by another investigator in 1836. Since the 1880s international conferences have been held from time to time for the purpose of establishing uniform standards of anthropometric procedures.

Military agencies had been taking stature measurements of recruits for many years, but around the time of the American Civil War anthropologists were carrying out exhaustive anthropometric surveys of military personnel, one of the first studies of large groups of living subjects. As early as 1853 daguerreotypic and photographic records were kept on native American populations.[54] The earliest extensive survey of biological variations of a European population has been attributed to the Prussian pathologist Rudolf Virchow (1821-1902), beginning in 1876. This work was initiated as a reaction to claims made by the French anthropologist de Quatrefages during the Franco-Prussian War that Germans had descended from dark-haired, brown-eyed Mongol barbarians.

Apart from demonstrating a greater number of variable characters in the biological constitution of mankind than had been formerly considered, this passion for measuring human bones and bodies was a reflection of some new insights into man's evolution. For one thing, human populations were recognized as having biological histories that could be reconstructed in part by comparative studies with prehistoric skeletal material. Secondly, traditional classifications of *sapiens* into a few racial groups seemed to be inadequate. Thirdly, evolutionary processes affecting human populations and producing variation of physique must be highly complex. The investigation of hybridization, acclimatization, and growth differences were viewed within the evolutionary framework. And finally, human variation was being in-

terpreted in the context of the social philosophy that particular native populations must be living representatives of past *stages* of human development on the road to progress. To many nineteenth-century anthropologists it seemed reasonable to attempt a reconstruction of a universal culture history on the basis of ethnographic data. This approach gained the respectability of a name—the *comparative method*. Such were the interests of the American lawyer Henry Lewis Morgan (1818-1881) who classified cultures within a threefold scheme of Savagery, Barbarism, and Civilization.[55] Where cultural development was lowly, the physical traits of a population were often assumed to be retarded or primitive as well.

Outside of anthropology itself, other kinds of evidence of cultural and geographical changes among peoples without written history were pressed into service. When Sir William Jones (1746-1794) demonstrated that Sanskrit, the tongue of the legendary Aryans of North India, had philological affinities to Persian, Latin, Greek, and a number of other ancient and modern languages (including English), it seemed only reasonable that there had been migrations of tribes carrying these languages from their places of origin to widely separated parts of the world.[56] Languages, like cultures and biological variations, were ranked according to reputed levels of development. Linguistics was also influential in the establishment of racial histories for particular populations, especially within Europe.

It was the recovery of a human fossil record with associated archeological data that was most welcome to evolutionists seeking to establish racial histories. Finds of prehistoric human skeletons had been made in Europe as early as 1700, but it was not until 1856 with the recovery of a Neanderthal skeleton near

54. A. Irving Hallowell, "The Beginnings of Anthropology in America," in *Selected Papers from the American Anthropologist 1888-1920*, ed. Frederica de Laguna (Evanston, Ill.: Row, Peterson and Company, 1960), pp. 1-90.

55. Henry Lewis Morgan, *Ancient Society: Researches in the Lines of Human Progress from Savagery through Barbarism to Civilization* (New York: World Publishing Company, 1877).

56. William Jones, *Asiatic Researches* (London: Royal Asiatic Society, 1786).

Düsseldorf, Germany, that scientific attention was drawn to the paleontological evidence for man's antiquity. This important discovery was followed by finds of other Neanderthal specimens in Europe, many of them in direct association with the bones of animals known to have become extinct in this part of the world since the final stages of the Pleistocene epoch, some ten thousand to eighty thousand years ago. Another kind of early man was found at Cro-Magnon in France in 1868, followed by more discoveries of the same sort of fossil hominid. While Neanderthals were originally assigned to a separate species on the basis of a strikingly low cranial vault, large brow ridges, and projecting face, the Cro-Magnon-like skeletons were recognized as being anatomically modern and therefore of the species *sapiens*. They also lived at a time after the extinction of Neanderthals, their archeological sites yielding artifacts that would not be confused with those of their predecessors.

There were efforts to relate these men of the Pleistocene to living races. Huxley noted the affinities of Neanderthals to Australian aborigines, while de Quatrefages sought the descendants of Cro-Magnon specimens among the modern populations of Europe. Then, in 1891, parts of a still more ancient human ancestor were found in Java, a creature named *Pithecanthropus*. At last the evolutionists had paleontological documentation that man had undergone modification of his physical features in the course of his evolutionary history, and Huxley's interpretation of comparative anatomy of apes and men was vindicated.

Given these paleontological data and the accumulating information about biological variations of modern populations that was encouraged by anthropometric analysis, it is not surprising that racial classifications became elaborated and cast in a configuration that was two-dimensional. Factors of space and time in human variation were obvious to a number of writers on this topic of which the most influential were the Russian-born French anthropologist Joseph Deniker (1852-1918) and his American colleague William Zebina Ripley (1867-1941), both of whom organized racial classifications for Europeans. Deniker identified ten races of Europe;[57] Ripley listed three.[58] The cephalic index played a major part in their classifications. Into the use of the index had crept the bias that dolichocephalism was superior to brachycephalism with respect to an assumed correlation of cranial form to levels of intellect. Elaborations of racial classifications for non-Europeans developed more slowly and never reached the degree of complexity characterizing those invented for the people of Europe. Linguistic and geographical elements colored racial classifications as did nationalistic and class differences.

The study of human variation in the second half of the nineteenth century turned to other observations that were not anthropometric in the narrow sense. Differential growth patterns of children, generational changes in the physical features of migrant populations, rates of fertility and viability of descendants, and related demographic problems were all considered. But implicit in this approach was the notion that racial purity was a reality and that it was worth preserving. Interracial unions were held to be harmful to members of all races. This was not a new idea, but now statistical methods were employed to either support or negate these claims. Much so-called anthropological lore was anecdotal yet offered up in scientific jargon. The same bias is seen in acclimatization studies, the difficulties of temperate populations living in tropical habitats being cited to support the thesis that racial differences were more than skin deep. These premises are essentially polygenetic, and their prevalence in late nineteenth-century anthropology is summed up by a contemporary historian of the discipline as follows.

The polygenist elements in late nineteenth-century European physical anthropology are evident in the characteristic preoccupations of its major figures; the assumption that the cultural differences of men were the direct product of differences in their racial physical structure; the idea that the distinguishing physical differences between human races were virtually primordial; the idea that the most important of these differences were those involving the human skull and brain;

57. Joseph Deniker, *The Races of Man* (New York: Charles Scribner, 1900).

58. William Zebina Ripley, *The Races of Europe: a Sociological Study* (New York: D. Appleton, 1899).

and the assumption that out of the heterogeneity of modern populations there could be reconstructed 'types' which were representative of the 'pure races' from whose mixture these modern populations derived.[59]

This survival of polygenesis within the framework of nineteenth-century evolutionary biology did not seem to be in conflict with the concept of natural selection. Indeed, it was thought that the operation of this mechanism explained how Europeans had succeeded to their present state of political dominance, an article of faith fundamental to the philosophy of *Social Darwinism* as proclaimed by Spencer. While Darwin expressed surprise that his biological treatise on species was employed by social philosophers to demonstrate that superior races were the products of natural selection, many of those persons who accepted the doctrine of progress and organic evolution saw these two ideas as logical correlates of the same natural law. "Survival of the fittest" was a phrase applied to society as well as biology. History more than biology was to provide the clues as to where a population stood in the scale of progress.

To preserve the superior qualities of the "better endowed races," Francis Galton (1822-1911) proposed in a publication of 1869 that natural selection be imitated by man in the selective breeding of individuals whose desirable mental and moral traits would ensure the betterment of future generations. This policy he called *eugenics,* and it had a tremendous appeal on both sides of the Atlantic.[60]

Darwin did not explain the formation of human races on the basis of natural selection. He looked to another evolutionary mechanism, sexual selection. In the *Descent of Man* Darwin wrote about the role of preferential mating among different animal species, then went on to describe how this behavior pattern served to diversify mankind since the time of his descent from some ancient ape ancestor in Africa. This book of 1871 is a work that its author claimed he wrote to meet the charge of some critics that he lacked courage in applying his evolutionary arguments to man's place in nature. Much of the information contained in the book is based upon Huxley's earlier essays on comparative anatomy and the fossil record as well as upon geological and archeological evidence of early man described in Lyell's *Geological Evidences of the Antiquity of Man.*[61] Darwin accounted for mental differences in man in a different way than natural or sexual selection, namely by the influence of culture. He wrote that virtuous moral qualities in human behavior were founded upon reason and such were adaptive aspects for human survival. These qualities were also products of natural selection. This separation of causes leading to mental and physical differences in man was not an important concept in anthropological theory until the twentieth century.

For Further Reading

Coleman, William. *Biology in the Nineteenth Century: Problems of Form, Function and Transformation.* New York: John Wiley and Sons, 1971. The chapters entitled *Transformation* (IV) and *Man* (V) discuss scientific and social thought relating to the rise of organic evolution as a theory.

Gillispie, Charles C. *Genesis and Geology: a Study of the Relations of Scientific Thought, Natural Theology and Social Opinion in Great Britain, 1790-1859.* New York: Harper and Brothers, 1959. The formation of concepts about geological processes and the age of the earth are discussed in this study of social and theological precepts in pre-Darwinian England.

Haller, John S. "Race and the Concept of Progress in Nineteenth Century American Ethnology," *American Anthropologist* 73 (1971): 710-724. This article discusses how the study of culture in the last century was effected by notions of racial superiority wherein non-Western peoples were considered outside the mainstream of evolutionary progress (i.e., they were thought to be survivals from the ancient past).

59. George W. Stocking, Jr., *Race, Culture and Evolution* (New York: Free Press, 1968), p. 56.

60. Francis Galton, *Hereditary Genius: an Inquiry into Its Laws and Consequences* (New York: Horizon, 1952).

61. Charles Lyell, *The Geological Evidences of the Antiquity of Man with Remarks on Theories of the Origin of Species by Variation* (London: John Murray, 1863).

Kennedy, Kenneth A. R. "Race and Culture," in *Main Currents in Cultural Anthropology,* ed. R. Naroll and F. Naroll. New York: Appleton-Century-Crofts, 1973, pp. 123-155. This chapter discusses the cultural background of the evolution of the race concept in Europe and America.

Odum, Herbert H. "Generalizations on Race in 19th Century Anthropology," *Isis* 58 (1967): 5-18. Various environmentalist theories of race formation are reviewed and compared.

Stanton, William *The Leopard's Spots: Scientific Attitudes towards Race in America, 1815-59.* Chicago: University of Chicago, 1960. This is an analysis of the polygenesis concept advocated by a number of American writers prior to the outbreak of the Civil War.

Bibliography

Darnell, Regna, ed. 1974. *Readings in the History of Anthropology.* New York: Harper & Row.

Haller, John S. 1971. *Outcasts from Evolution: Scientific Attitudes of Racial Inferiority, 1859-1900.* Urbana: University of Illinois.

Quade, Lawrence G. 1971. *American Physical Anthropology: a Historical Perspective,* Doctoral Dissertation at the University of Kansas, 1967. Ann Arbor, Mich.: University Microfilms (Xerox Company).

4 | Evolution of Ancient and Living Populations

SOURCES OF GENETIC DIVERSITY

Until almost a generation after the discovery of Mendel's laws of inheritance in 1900, it was thought that genetics and Darwinian evolution were incompatible areas of inquiry.[1] A controversy began in the latter part of the nineteenth century between those biologists faithful to Darwin's idea that organic evolution was a gradual process with natural selection operating upon minor hereditary variations and their opponents, who argued that evolutionary changes were marked by discontinuity and abrupt mutative leaps. Supporters of these two camps were labeled *biometricians* and *Mendelians* respectively.[2] Members of the latter party came to recognize, as a consequence of their own experimental work, that genetic mutation theory was compatible, after all, with what Darwin's followers had to say, and a synthesis of these two developments, which are integral to modern evolutionary theory, was accomplished in the early 1930s.[3] Genetics became a rapidly specialized field with subfields forming in plant genetics, medical genetics, and population genetics, of which the last is of primary interest to us.

Characters studied by the geneticist are structural (anatomical), functional (physiological), and behavioral (ethological). But not all characters that show variability and mutability are heritable. *Nongenetic* variation is exemplified by loss of a limb as the result of an accident or disease and by alterations of

stature and body form that attend advancement in age. Variables of this sort are not transformed into the genetic system, hence they are not perpetuated in populations. However, the effects of environmental stresses on nongenetic variables may be as profound as those effecting genetic variables. The notion that acquired characters could become inherited persisted until August Weismann's (1834-1914) experiments on rat pedigrees at the end of the nineteenth century forced skeptics to abandon this ancient superstition.

Traits attributable to an individual's genetic system constitute his *genotype*. This is a com-

---

1. In 1866 Mendel published a paper on his research on the genetics of garden peas in a journal of the Natural History Society of Brno, Czechoslovakia. His valuable work was discovered in 1900 by three investigators who had come independently to the same conclusions about the laws of inheritence as Mendel had done so many years earlier. These geneticists were Hugo de Vries (1848-1935) of the Netherlands, Karl Erich Correns (1864-1933) of Germany, and Erich Tschermak von Seysenegg (1871-1962) of Austria.

2. Karl Pearson (1857-1936), who gave the name *biometry* to the study of heredity, is associated with the application of statistics to biological problems. The Mendelian school was advanced by Galton, discussed above, and by William Bates (1861-1926). All were Englishmen.

3. The research of Ronald A. Fisher (1890-1962), John Burdon Sanderson Haldane (1892-1964), and Sewell Wright (1889-   ) are discussed in terms of this historical wedding of scientific approaches to evolution in Julian S. Huxley, *Evolution: the Modern Synthesis* (New York: Harper and Brothers, 1942).

plex molecular organization containing the units of inheritance called *genes*. All cells of the body possess genes, but it is the set of specialized sex cells (*gametes*) of the reproductive organs that function to pass on the combination of genetic constitutions of male and female parents to their offspring after mating and fertilization have taken place. The structure of genes is referred to as DNA (deoxyribonucleic acid molecule), which has the capacity to replicate itself in the nuclei of cells. The basis of individuality is the presence of long chains of amino acids in various sequences that are called *proteins*. These are of different types, each capable of controlling a particular body characteristic. There are a great number of proteins, and all functions of an individual are dependent upon their specific activities. Their presence is detected by a technique called *electrophoresis* where an electric field is applied to a group of proteins. Different electrical charges of proteins exposed to this environment are registered when the proteins move apart and migrate at specific rates within the electric field. This is a very useful method for studying genetic differences, for if one amino acid is substituted by another in the amino acid chain of the DNA molecule, then its mobility in the electrophoretic scan will be easily observable. A substitution of this kind is evidence of a genetic variation. The gene is a shorthand expression for the segment of DNA molecule responsible for the synthesis of a particular protein. DNA molecules are formed as a double-coiled helix. DNA forms another molecular product called RNA (ribonucleic acid) that in the form of a single chain passes into the area of the cell outside the nucleus and acts as a synthesizer of proteins.

The physical manifestation of an individual's genotype is called the *phenotype*. Blue eyes, for example, are the phenotypic expression of those genes that determine eye color. Dark eyes indicate the action of other genes for his variable. Phenotypic characters may be expressed as *continuous* traits, as when a variable feature is described as larger or smaller, darker or lighter, or rougher or smoother. Continuous genetic traits are often the expression of many genes (i.e., they are *polygenic*). *Discontinuous* characters, such as the presence or absence of an inheritable disease, wavy or

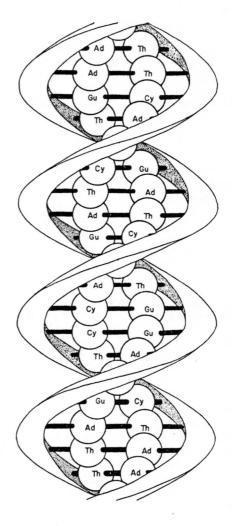

FIGURE 4.1. Schematic representation of the structure of DNA, based upon the model proposed by J. D. Watson and F. H. C. Crick in 1953. Nucleotides shown here are molecules containing the nitrogen bases adenine (Ad), thymine (Th), guanine (Gu), and cytosine (Cy). These constitute sugar phosphate chains in this diagram of the double helix with its hydrogen bonds. From Bruce Wallace, **Chromosomes, Giant Molecules and Evolution.** New York: W. W. Norton, 1966, p. 98, fig. 10.

spiral hair form, or a blood type, are discrete features that may be the phenotypic expressions of the action of a single gene or a small number of genes. The occurrence of variable expressions of a trait within a species is called *polymorphism*. All genetic characteristics that distinguish populations from one another are polymorphic. Through the study of family pedigrees in man and through breeding experiments in animals it is possible to discover if a particular characteristic is a phenotypic expression of a genotype or is of nongenetic origin.

The study of heredity must begin with the individual who is the temporary depository of a small portion of the genes present in his population. An individual may directly affect the *gene pool* of his population if he is especially prolific and so contributes more of his genes to future generations than individuals leaving fewer offspring. Or he may make a novel, but involuntary, contribution of a new gene of which he would be the first carrier. This would be a *mutant gene*. Failure to produce offspring is the withholding of a potential genetic contribution, as occurs in cases of celibacy and infertility. The proving ground of the genes of an individual is the breeding population, for here all genetic contributions will be tested for their capacity to survive in interaction with the genes of other breeding members of the population.

While the genetic nature of the individual is static at any moment, a population is constantly changing through time. In fact, evolution could be defined as a change in the genetic composition of populations. No two individuals are alike, not even identical twins sharing the same genotype. Therefore populations are not genetically the same either. When geneticists refer to *population* in a genetic context they mean the local or breeding group, the reservoir from which the totality of genes for an assembly of individuals is contained. Sometimes called the *deme*, this breeding population is assumed to be randomly interbreeding (i.e., composed of individuals so situated that any two of them have equal probability of mating with each other and producing offspring, providing, of course, that the partners are sexually mature, of opposite sex, and equivalent with respect to their availability

and receptivity as mates). The deme is the unit of evolution.

Diversity of genetic constitutions is necessary for the survival of a population, as Darwin so well understood in defining the importance of variants. The greater the diversity of genotypes within a deme, the higher is the probability that the population will include those particular constitutions that will survive shifts in ecological settings, as with sudden changes in temperature or the need to exploit a new source of nutrients because of the disappearance of foods formerly available. Genetic variability also makes possible the geographical distribution of a population into new areas, thus extending the habitat necessary for the support of life.

Evolution is opportunistic, and at the level of gene action we can define a number of stages where variability is introduced. Not only are genes themselves diverse in their molecularity, but their positions in linear order on strands of nucleoproteins, called *chromosomes,* within the nucleus of the gametes are inconstant. When these sex cells divide, which is their method of reproduction, there is a reshuffling of chromosomes which makes daughter cells different, a process called *meiotic cell division.* This does not occur in the body (*somatic*) cells, which duplicate themselves exactly in a different reproductive process, called *mitotic cell division.*

While the number of chromosomal strands is constant for a species from generation to generation (man has twenty-three paired chromosomes), irregularities of chromosomal structure may lead to further genetic variation. Genes act differently in the presence of other genes. This was known to Mendel who noted that when one gene is inactive in the presence of another gene of the same pair, the result is *recessive* (i.e., this gene will not be manifested phenotypically). The other gene is *dominant,* and its quality is phenotypically expressed. Like-genes on the same locus on the chromosome (*homozygous* condition) may be either recessive or dominant; *heterozygous* conditions exist when there is one recessive and one dominant gene on the same loci of the chromosomal pair. A dominant gene in either homozygous or heterozygous combination with its paired gene will be expressed phenotypically.

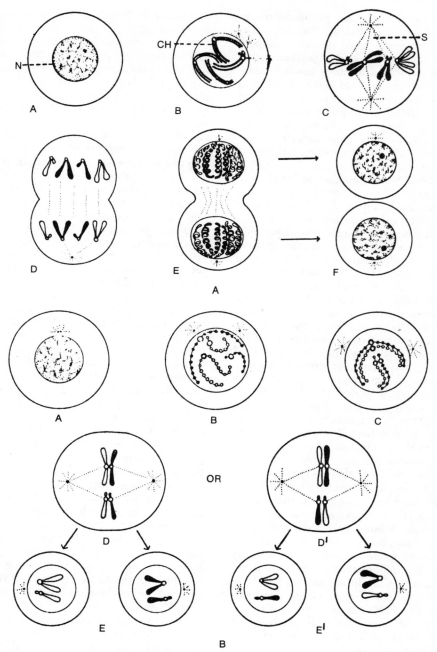

FIGURE 4.2. Cell division of **mitosis** (A) and **meiosis** (B). N = nucleus; CH = chromosome; S = spindle along which chromosomal alignment occurs. Meiotic cell division is represented here with **dark** paternal chromosomes and **light** maternal chromosomes. Adapted from Kurt Stern, **Principles of Human Genetics.** 2nd edition. San Francisco: Freeman, 1960, pp. 14 and 64, figs. 6 and 34.

Mendel worked out the basic principles of single-gene inheritance, making the important discovery that genes may operate independently of one another. Today we know that some genes are linked to other genes because of their loci on the same chromosome. Also a single gene may bring about several different phenotypic characters, a phenomenon called *pleiotropy*. The degree of phenotypic expression, or *penetrance*, of a gene varies considerably between individuals possessing the same character genotypically.

Fertilization presents another order of complexity to the evolution of variability. There is a randomness in the union of male and female gametes in every fertilization. Since meiosis insures that no two gametes are alike, children of the same parents are also unlike, save in the case of identical twins who develop from a single *ovum* (female gamete) fertilized by a single *sperm cell* (male gamete). Differences in identical twins are due to nongenetic factors. So-called *fraternal twins* are offspring conceived simultaneously when two different ova are fertilized by two different sperm cells. After the sperm cell penetrates the cell wall of the ovum and fertilization is effected, the new cellular entity, the *zygote,* must be viable and survive in the early period of embryonic development. During the time of prenatal growth (*gestation*), the new individual will increase in body size by mitotic cell division, a process that leads to the production of some 3 trillion cells for a newborn human baby. As the embryonic cells multiply, they become specialized into tissues and organs. One such aggregate of cells form the gametes that, at the time of puberty, will assume a meiotic form of cell division. A human female will produce some 400 ova in a lifetime, usually one gamete maturing every month. The human male may emit some 200 million sperm cells in a single ejaculation, a total of approximately 1,650 billion sperm cells in a lifetime. Given this scope of gamete variability, it is obvious that the probabilities of any two individuals being genetically identical, except for monozygotic twins, is remote indeed!

Studies of pedigrees represent minute segments of breeding populations, and the proportions of genotypic and phenotypic distributions that these family studies provide are applicable to their populations as well. These ratios are treated as constants by the geneticist (i.e., every population is assumed to be in genetic equilibrium when mating occurs randomly and no new genes are entering or leaving the population). Under such hypothetical circumstances all generations of the same population would have genotypic and phenotypic proportions that are the same. This concept is called the *Hardy-Weinberg Equilibrium* after the two men who formulated it in 1908.[4] It is one of the cornerstones of modern population genetics. The simple algebraic formula expressing this equilibrium enables the geneticist to compute the frequency of a given gene in a gene pool when data derived from pedigree studies or populational surveys is available for an assessment of phenotypic frequencies. Any effects of inbreeding that may temporarily upset gene frequencies will be corrected after a single generation of random mating. However, it is obvious that various influences of a genetic and nongenetic nature *do* alter the gene pools of populations with the result that modern populations are different from their ancestral populations in the frequencies of particular genes. It has been the continuous accumulation of minor genetic changes over time that has brought forth *Homo sapiens* from ancestral populations that the fossil record reveals to have been different. Yet this change has not been abrupt. It is the result of minor and discrete genetic changes that appeared in populations from one generation to the next, small effects that we refer to as *microevolutionary*. Such effects disrupt the equilibrium of populations and thus are seen as additional causes for human diversity.

Environmental circumstances may prevail whereby a particular gene undergoes a radical transformation called a *mutation*. Mutated genes are one way in which new genetic material is introduced to a gene pool. What takes place at the biochemical level may be a molecular alteration within the DNA molecule itself or a change in chromosomal activity. We do not know all the causes for mutation, but they can be induced experimentally with laboratory animals whose reproductive organs are

4. Godfrey Harold Hardy, "Mendelian Proportions in a Mixed Population," *Science* 28 (1908):49-50.

exposed to X rays and to various radioactive materials. It has been suggested that certain viruses may be involved in the triggering of mutations. Mutation is an "accidental" process (i.e., gene and chromosome alterations of this kind are random). They offer no guarantee of survival value to the individual producing them or to his offspring. Cataracts, brachyphalangy (abnormally broad and short fingers), syndactyly (fusion of fingers), certain kinds of dwarfism, and hemophilia are malfunctions in man that must be attributed to the action of mutated genes. Mutations may bring about the death of an organism before reproductive age is reached, in which case the genes are lost and do not enter the gene pool. Most mutations are harmful for they interfere with those genetic operations that have become predominant through the process of natural selection. On the other hand, all genes have histories of mutation, for such are the raw materials of evolutionary change. In such cases a dominant gene may become recessive, a recessive gene dominant, or a completely different gene may appear on a locus where a homozygous pair of genes had existed before. If a new gene appears that benefits an individual, his chance for survival is increased with respect to its phenotypic trait. In time the new gene may become intrinsic to the success of his population once it is introduced into the gene pool. Both favorable and unfavorable mutations may be critical to a population's biological success generations after they have been introduced. Such cryptic mutated genes may remain preadaptive to conditions that later become optimal for survival.

Since deleterious genes would appear to be unfavorable for survival, we may ask why they persist in populations. Might natural selection operate to preserve a lethal mutation? One example of *adaptive mutation* in man is the case of sickle-cell anemia, which occurs in high frequency in people of West African descent. This disease is caused by a recessive gene that predisposes an individual's red blood cells to become distorted under certain circumstances. The sickle-shaped cell is not inherited as such but is the result of a metabolic defect which is of genetic origin. The homozygous presence of this gene causes death, usually in the early teens. Heterozygous presence of the same gene

means that the carrier may be ill from the disease, but probabilities are high that this will not be the cause of his death. It has been discovered from genetic research in Africa that the persons who possess the sickle-cell gene in heterozygous form are protected from a quite different disease which is nongenetically acquired—malaria. Persons lacking the sickle-cell gene are prone to suffer more severely from the debilitating effects of malaria. Thus it was observed that the presence of the sickling gene in heterozygous form is an adaptive polymorphism whose high frequency in malarial areas of Africa is due to natural selection. In areas without malaria, the sickling gene is absent.[5] Where balanced polymorphisms of this kind exist, they depend upon heterozygote superiority: otherwise the better-adapted genes will become fixed in a population through the operation of natural selection.

Another way a population can increase its degree of genetic variability is to receive genes from an already existing gene pool of the same species. The formation of new genotypic combinations is due to this phenomena called *gene flow*. This may or may not be a reciprocal process between populations. An example of one-way gene flow is the Spanish and Portuguese settlement of Latin America where native American populations received a high proportion of European genes, but Spain and Portugal were not significantly modified by genes from the New World. Two-way gene flow is represented today in many parts of the United States, especially in urban areas. Migrated genes may bestow greater adaptability to the recipients, since these genes have already undergone selective sorting elsewhere. Gene flow is a normal activity for all human groups, but its occurrence may be higher along border areas between the habitats of macropopulations. Since man belongs to a single species, all populations being interfertile, we must suppose that effective reproductive isolating mechanisms have never existed in the course of our species' biological history. Mechanisms

5. Anthony C. Allison, "The Distribution of the Sickle-Cell Trait in East Africa and Elsewhere and Its Apparent Relationship to the Incidence of Subterian Malaria," *Transactions of the Royal Society of Tropical Medicine and Hygiene* 48 (1954):312-318.

that inhibit gene flow in human populations are geographical and cultural, not biological. Two populations may live side by side for generations without any significant exchange of genes. The practice of in-group marriage (*endogamy*) is one cultural mechanism that can reinforce the restriction of gene flow. Languages and religions are other barriers, although never impenetrable. Examples of culturally isolating factors are seen in the genetic separation of Lapps and their Scandinavian neighbors, in African pygmies and those settled agriculturalists and cattle herders surrounding their forest habitats, or in American white and Asiatic populations in California until quite recent times. Caste groups in India are also endogamous, and Gypsies have retained a high degree of genetic isolation and cultural identity in some parts of the world where they have settled.

Genetic equilibrium is most effectively maintained in human groups when the size of the population is large. When a census falls below 1000 persons or so, not all of whom can be active contributors to the gene pool, certain genes from the parental gene pool will be represented in lower frequency or be entirely lost. In other words, genes will be shared by proportionally more people in a small splinter group than in the macropopulation from whence it was originally derived. A mutated gene will have a stronger effect upon the former population, since there are proportionally more offspring to be affected by it. Therefore, if the small population is prevented from backcrossing with members of the parental population or from members of other gene pools, after a few generations it will form its own "private" gene pool with gene frequencies that distinguish it from other populations. This evolutionary process is called *genetic drift*. Small population size and reproductive isolation are the conditions under which this process may take place.

Drift is another evolutionary mechanism. If reproductive isolation continues over a period of to time, a population may evolve reproductive isolating mechanisms that separate it completely from the larger population from which it was originally derived. Perhaps in the prehistoric past, genetic drift played a significant role in the evolution of our species when hunting bands of fifty or so individuals were isolated from other bands for long periods of time, although never long enough to lead to speciation. The absence of blood type B among native Americans before 1492 may be due to the fact that their Asiatic ancestors entered the New World in small bands that were high in O and lacked B genes. The presence of the gene for blood type A in native Americans of the great plains, but not in other parts of the New World, again suggests the operation of drift. Drift has been studied in religious isolates whose matings have been endogamous for several generations and whose genetic isolation from the parental populations have continued over several generations. Studies of Dunker and Hutterite communities in this country have provided some interesting insights into the consequences of drift. For example, their blood type frequencies and certain morphological features of the body too, appear in different frequencies from what is found in the German populations to which they are related. Their gene frequencies are different as well from the American population, thus we think that it is drift rather than gene flow that is a major cause for their genetic differences.[6] Other studies of drift operating in contemporary human groups have been carried out. All efforts to discern drift must take into account a number of variables: the rate of gene flow that has taken place in the past or is presently occurring, the length of time the population has been isolated, and whether or not the original isolates were genetically random or were selected on the basis of their phenotypic characters.[7]

To determine if a population has been affected by the mechanism of drift, it is necessary to discover if the genes under consideration are directly related to the group's

6. Bentley Glass, M. S. Sacks, E. F. John, and C. Hess, "Genetic Drift in a Religious Isolate: an Analysis of the Causes of Variation in Blood Group and Other Gene Frequencies in a Small Population," *American Naturalist* 86 (1952):145-159. Some geneticists discount drift as a significant evolutionary factor.

7. Sewell Wright, "Evolution in Mendelian Populations," *Genetics* 16 (1931):97-159 and idem, "On the Role of Directed and Random Changes in Gene Frequency in the Genetics of Populations," *Evolution* 2 (1948):279-294.

adaptation to its habitat and way of life. If adaptability appears to be involved, then natural selection is more likely to be the cause for their frequency. It is difficult to identify adaptive characteristics in man where we are unable to demonstrate the possible survival value of traits that appear randomly and do not seem critical to the biological success of a population. Many so-called "neutral genes" held up as illustrative of the operation of drift have turned out to be adaptive when more was learned about them.

The evolutionary mechanism called the *founder effect* refers to the circumstances of small isolates being established by individuals. Their genotypes may have been rare in the macropopulation from whence they came, but they become a predominant feature of the isolate as its numbers increase. In human populations of historic times, cases of the founder effect can be documented from written records.

Genetic drift alone cannot bring about major evolutionary changes. This is the role of natural selection that operates upon an isolated group from the moment of its separation from the major population. Survival is measured in terms of those organisms that live to reproduce themselves and not simply measured in the number of births occurring in a population at a given time or in the size of a population. Natural selection is a guiding and stabilizing force in evolution, since it works upon the effects of other mechanisms. It is a conservative process that checks the potential for unlimited variation brought about by gene assortment, mutation, and gene flow. Natural selection has been described as nature's arbiter, while adaptation is the mediator between an organism and its environment. Mutation and drift are random with regard to adaptation, and gene flow can do little more than compensate for the effects of drift. Variations of pigmentation, body form, biochemistry, metabolism, and the host of other phenotypic features of polygenic or single gene inheritance in man are the consequences of natural selection. The targets of natural selection do not remain the same over time. Here the prehistoric skeletal record may provide important data for the investigation of selective pressures

on our species from ancient times to the present.

Does sexual selection operate in human evolution? Darwin thought so, assigning to this mechanism the origin of human races. Anthropologists asking this question have become aware that standards of mate selection are different in all societies, yet these do not significantly affect the abilities of most individuals to find mates and have offspring with the sexually more attractive members of their societies. Furthermore, standards of beauty change, as a comparison of Ruben's buxom nudes and recent award winners in Atlantic City demonstrate.

GEOGRAPHICAL DISTRIBUTION OF HUMAN POLYMORPHISMS

If anthropology had come into its own as a field of scientific inquiry *after* 1900, its approach to questions of human variation would have been set from the beginning by the concepts of genetics. But anthropologists had been around for several generations before the year Mendel's laws of inheritance were discovered, by which time anthropometry dominated the older discipline as a technique for describing man's biological diversity and assigning populations to racial classifications. It was not until 1950 with the publication of *Genetics and the Races of Man: an Introduction to Modern Physical Anthropology* by William C. Boyd (1903-   ) that a text was available that applied the principles of genetics to a field preoccupied with older methodologies.[8] Boyd did not reject the idea of racial classification for man, but he urged his readers to leave anthropometry in its proper place in forensic, demographic, and applied studies: questions about human variation and taxonomy should be put in a form that would concentrate upon those polymorphisms of discernible genetic basis. Boyd favored the use of serological polymorphisms, since they appeared to be free from selective pressures and hence were nonadaptive. To discover

8. William C. Boyd, *Genetics and the Races of Man: an Introduction to Modern Physical Anthropology* (Boston: Little, Brown and Company, 1950).

the genes producing such traits and to plot their geographical distribution would, Boyd promised, provide a superior means of formulating meaningful racial taxonomies than had resulted from all previous efforts based upon the measurement of polygenic traits of uncertain genetic basis.

Boyd's book found a receptive audience, bringing problems about human diversity into a field that had been approached but not yet entered by geneticists looking at nonhuman species.[9] Meanwhile, the German-born American anthropologist Franz Boas (1858-1942) had made it clear that polygenic features of body size and cranial form underwent considerable modifications among immigrants from Europe and their descendants living in the United States. These differences were observed to increase in proportion to the length of time parents had lived in their new country. Boas's study indicated that environment played some part in bodily changes.[10] Similar findings were obtained by Boas's younger colleague, Harry Shapiro (1902-   ), who compared Japanese-Hawaiians, their offspring, and the relatives who had remained in Japan.[11] Studies of individuals becoming adaptively modified to their environments during growth —a phenomenon called *plasticity*—led a number of anthropologists to supplement anthropometric descriptions with reports of traits that were not so responsive to environmental influences. Traits of known genetic character thus came to be valued, extremists of this new approach going so far as to disregard all anthropometric data.

Counter to this radical view and to Boyd's search for traits determined by "neutral genes" devoid of adaptive significance is a fact long known to geneticists: gene activity is comprehensible only in terms of the environmental situation in which the genotype is expressed phenotypically. Natural selection operates upon the phenotype, not upon the genes per se. Therefore a study of diversity in any population must include (1) examination of those traits recognizable as phenotypic expressions of either single gene or polygenic inheritance, and (2) the analysis of all observable characters within the geographical range of the species with respect to their adaptive significance. With these two points in view, three American anthropologists published an innovative study of human variability that appeared the same year as did the book by Boyd. This is *Races: a Study of the Problems of Race Formation in Man.*[12] Revised editions of this important work have subsequently appeared under the name of one of its authors, but with a different title. However, the ecological orientation of the 1950 edition has been retained.[13]

Anthropometric studies of body size and form have served to demonstrate ways in which natural selection has operated in the full geographical range of *Homo sapiens*. Extremes of world temperatures range from above 130 degrees F. in the shade in desert regions to below minus 70 degrees F. in the Arctic. In certain desert areas, soil temperatures shift from 125 degrees F. at noon to below freezing at night. Man has adapted to these stresses in a number of ways, both biologically and culturally, even attaining high levels of culture in inhospitable habitats. Among the most obvious of physical adaptations to thermal stress is body size. Small people are found in highest frequency in tropical regions, large people in colder areas of the temperate zone. One factor of body size is weight, which tends to be lower in regions of high mean annual temperatures. Nutritional stress must be considered a factor of body size too, for in areas where famine is common and a caloric intake below 800 units per day is habitual, the growth potential of individuals will not be realized. On the other hand, overnutrition would be of selective disadvantage

9. Theodosius Dobzhansky, *Genetics and the Origin of Species* (New York: Columbia University, 1937): Ernst Mayr, *Systematics and the Origin of Species* (New York: Columbia University, 1942).

10. Franz Boas, "Changing Bodily Form of Descendants of Immigrants," *American Anthropologist* 14 (1912):530-562.

11. Harry Shapiro, *Migration and Environment: a Study of the Physical Characteristics of the Japanese Immigrants to Hawaii and the Effects of Environment on their Descendants* (London: Oxford University, 1939).

12. Carleton S. Coon, Stanley M. Garn, and Joseph Birdsell, *Races: a Study of the Problems of Race Formation in Man* (Springfield, Ill.: Charles C. Thomas, 1950).

13. Stanley M. Garn, *Human Races*, 3rd ed. (Springfield, Ill.: Charles C. Thomas, 1971).

in the hotter parts of the world, placing a strain upon metabolic activities.

Biogeographers have known for years that desert-adapted varieties of a species tend toward linearity of body form, while Arctic varieties have a lower surface-mass ratio. Many Arctic animals, including seals and polar bears, have this latter type of body form. This feature is apparent as well in a reduction of limb size in relation to the size of the trunk, and in an abbreviation of other body projections. Related to this body form is the presence of an insulating layer of fat. Eskimos, too, have short limbs and long trunks in combination with an adipose layer of some thickness, although these people are not necessarily fat. The reduction of body surface to mass in Arctic species insures that less heat is lost by convection, conduction, or radiation. Shorter body projections allow for a greater capacity to remain warm and avoid the risk of frostbite. In addition to these biological adaptations, Eskimos have fatty deposits in the region of their cheekbones and about their orbits, narrow eye openings with a high frequency of epicanthic folds, and reduction of nasal projection. They also show increased metabolic responses to cold providing that they are well nourished. Some of these same features are found among other cold-adapted peoples, such as the Indians living in high altitudes in the Andes.

In contrast to the cold-adapted phenotypic pattern of body build are those peoples living in dry desert areas of high temperature. They have body forms that maximize surface relative to mass with consequent loss of heat through sweating. Their bodies are linear and the extremities are long in relation to trunk size. Fat is not adaptive in this ecological setting. Under hot, humid conditions dark skin may have a selective advantage in initiating more rapid sweating through elevation of body surface temperature. Darkest skins occur in sub-Saharan Africa, southern India, Melanesia, and Australia. Skin color is due in large part to the inherited capacity to produce the substance *melanin* under the stimulus of solar radiation. This pigment is produced in the dermal layers of the skin. Desert dwellers lack the amount of body hair found in peoples living in the cooler parts of the world. Forms of head hair vary from helical, or woolly, to spiral

tufts in Africa and Oceania. Straight hair is characteristic of Asiatic peoples and their relatives in the New World. European hair forms are usually wavy or curly with lower frequencies of straight hair. The form of the hair may be adaptive in certain regions, for spiral hair helps to keep the neck exposed, thereby causing a more efficient release of body heat by sweating. Straight hair, when grown to sufficient length, can protect and warm the neck in cold areas of the world where this hair form is found in highest frequency. In addition to these structural adaptations to thermal stress, we might add metabolic traits, which are also variable and adaptive. The cold nights that are experienced in deserts become tolerable with metabolic generation of more body heat, as is the case with the Kalihari Bushmen sleeping in the open and without warm clothing. You and I would resort to extra blankets and clothing under these conditions of night cold, but in time we would acquire some tolerance through our capacities for heightened metabolic activity, even during sleep, if deprived of these amenities.

Most features of human variation are less easy to explain in terms of their adaptive sig-

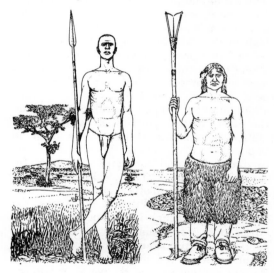

FIGURE 4.3. Comparison of body forms of a tropical East African and an arctic Eskimo. From William W. Howells, "The Distribution of Man," **Scientific American** 203 (1960): 2.

nificance. The *Wormian bones* along the cranial sutures are difficult to interpret, although we know that these accessory bones are related to factors of cranial growth. These bones appear in high frequency in native Americans and Asiatics. And how are the differences in consistency of *cerumen* (earwax) from the dry forms found in Asiatics to the sticky forms found in Africans and Europeans to be accounted for? Some variables in man are group-specific, such as fusion of certain bones of the wrist in peoples of African descent. *Steatopygia* (accumulation of adipose tissue on the buttocks) is peculiar to Bushmen and Hottentot females. The Papago Indians are unique in many dental features. On the other hand, the ABO blood group system is represented by some genes in all human populations.

This ABO system was the first of a succession of serological systems that have been found widely distributed in our species. Some blood groups are "private" systems shared by only a few individuals while others are worldwide. Each one has its particular pattern of distribution, thus demolishing any hopes that blood types alone can provide a basis of a racial taxonomy that would be superior to one founded on morphological variables. Thus the *Duffy-positive* gene has a frequency of 40 percent in England, is very rare in Africa, but is high in the Far East and the Pacific. A different blood group called *Diego* is essentially absent in Australia, rare among Alaskans, and most often present in Peruvian Indians, Chinese, Japanese, and Koreans. Genetic variations of other immunological traits include the defect in the synthesis of normal hemoglobin causing the disease *thalassemia* in populations living along the shores of the Mediterranean and eastwards into Iran, India, and Thailand. The sickle-cell trait of West Africa is another abnormal hemoglobin, are also of different genotypes; the form Hp^1 being high in Europe and parts of Africa, but not frequent in the Far East. A rare form called Hp^{2m} is absent in Europeans, but occurs in Africa and among persons of African descent in other parts of the world. Sensitivity to certain chemicals shows variability too. Phenylthiocarbamide (PTC) is one such substance that has a high number of tasters among native Americans, western Asiatics, and Afri-

cans, but surveys in Europe and India reveal high frequencies of nontasters.

It is in the area of abnormal functioning of the human body that many polymorphisms have been found. Among these are the diseases of *familial Mediterranean fever* and *favism*, the latter being an allergic reaction to the broad bean *Vicia fava*. Both diseases appear in high frequency among Europeans. *Tay-Sachs disease* is most common in Ashkinazic Jews, high in Sephardic Jews, but rare among their European non-Jewish neighbors, even within the area of the Polish-Russian border where it is most prevalent in Jewish communities. *Lactase deficiency*, or the inherited inability to tolerate milk due to lack of the lactase enzyme, is most common in Asia and Africa, but least common among Europeans. Another enzyme disease of genetic origin is *phenylketonuria* (PKU), which can cause brain damage in one out of every thousand births among Europeans. The frequency of PKU is lower in Japanese and seldom found among peoples of African origin. Chromosomal abnormalities, *cystic fibrosis,* and some forms of *diabetes* are of genetic origin and show varying frequencies in world populations.

Since 1950 there has been a shift away from the study of specific human variations and their geographical distributions to the investigation of populations. The anthropologist William W. Howells (1908-   ) has observed that

The emphasis is on the influences affecting the biological nature of populations, and the method, in general, is more precise definition of the population under study, and of exact details of its structure: degree of isolation, size, regional subgroups, age, sex, social, or economic divisions, mating patterns, and the whole environmental background. This contrasts with earlier work, which, often interested in classification, tended to generalize and typologize, blurring important minor distinctions and losing information by so doing. Much of recent work can be called microevolution, investigating small-scale differentiation and change in man: it makes much more use of theory and information from genetics and biology, and has more advanced statistical methods for testing and control.[14]

We have observed already an example of this move from description for its own sake to discernment of process in the study of sickle-cell disease in Africa. As it has been described by the American anthropologist Frank Livingstone (1928-   ), the gene for sickling became an adaptive polymorphism against the effects of malaria when early farmers some four or five thousand years ago moved into West Africa. Much of the continent had been free of malaria in terminal Pleistocene times when conditions for the breeding of the *Anopheles gambiae* mosquito did not exist. But with the formation of stagnant ponds of water forming in open fields, which were cut into the jungle by slash-and-burn cultivators, the malaria-carrying insects were able to find favorable breeding places. As human populations grew in size, the mosquitos found sufficient numbers of prey to insure their survival. In this case the process at work was cultural behavior influencing the ecology of an area and thus bringing about changes to the human populations.[15] It is probable that Neolithic agricultural techniques of slash-and-burn and the building of tanks for the storage of water that took place in the Mediterranean basin made the malarial situation there more acute than it had been previously in this humid and marshy terrain. If so, thalessemia may have become an adaptive polymorphism in this part of the world just as the sickling polymorphism took hold in Africa.

Racial classifications have continued to be of interest to some twentieth-century anthropologists. *The Races of Europe,* published in 1939 by Carleton S. Coon (1904-   ), contained a description of many racial divisions for this part of the world.[16] Earnest Albert Hooton (1887-1954), who trained an entire generation of anthropologists during his time at Harvard University, wrote about *primary races, secondary races,* and *composite races* in his famous text *Up From the Ape.*[17] More recently, Garn has listed nine geographical races defined by physical barriers to reproduction (in ancient times at least). Some thirty-two *local races,* which Garn considers to be the true evolutionary units, are included in the

geographical categories, but he observes that these do not represent all of the thousands of local races that are simply defined as tribes or as small breeding populations in a local area. To this system, Garn adds an unspecified number of *microraces,* smaller demographic groups within human settlements of larger size.[18] Along with these major works on racial anthropology, we should include Coon's books wherein five basic races are identified, each with several subdivisions.[19]

These recent studies include both anthropometric and genetic data, but the acceptance of the genetic approach by anthropologists earlier in this century was gradual. As late as 1923 Roland Burrage Dixon (1875-1934) of Harvard wrote that because of the difficulties in knowing the "unit factors" (genes) back of many morphological features, it was more expedient to turn to anthropometric measurements of gross (polygenic) structures. Indeed, Dixon believed that a combination of only three metrical calculations on the head were sufficient to detect racial differences for classificatory purposes. All possible combinations of these three basic observations, which were expressed as indices, led to the establishment of twenty-seven different races.[20] As we have noted, Boyd's major contribution to the study of human variation brought an end to nongenetic racial classifications. Today the value of both anthropometric and genetic data is recognized, and the incorporation of these procedures appears in texts after 1950.

By the early part of this century anthropologists had come far in appreciating the distinc-

14. William W. Howells, "Recent Physical Anthropology," *Annals of the American Academy of Political and Social Sciences* 389 (1970):116-126.

15. Frank Livingstone, "Anthropological Implications of Sickle Cell Gene Distribution in West Africa," *American Anthropologist* 60 (1958):533-562.

16. Carleton S. Coon, *The Races of Europe* (New York: Macmillan, 1939).

17. Earnest Albert Hooton, *Up From the Ape* (New York: Macmillan, 1931).

18. Garn, *Human Races.*

19. Carleton S. Coon, *The Origin of Races* (New York: Alfred A. Knopf, 1962) and Carleton S. Coon with Edward E. Hunt, Jr., *The Living Races of Man* (New York: Alfred A. Knopf, 1965).

20. Roland Burrage Dixon, *The Racial History of Man* (New York: Charles Scribner's Sons, 1923).

tive features of biological race, language, and culture. This awareness that biologically inherited traits are of a different order of phenomena than behavior that is acquired by learning through membership in a social group constitutes one of the major intellectual contributions of anthropology to modern science. In this principle, Boas trained his students who came to study with him at Clark University and later at Columbia at a time when he was the only full-time professor of anthropology in this country. His attitudes toward the discrete qualities of man's biology and his resistance to all racist propaganda have given a characteristic stamp to anthropology in America, even though some lesser known writers in Europe had earlier expressed their reservations about the assumption that race and culture were correlated.

Attempts to demonstrate that individuals and populations are significantly different in intelligence and temperament have not been conclusive. The possibility of devising a "culture free" test for the measurement of these qualities is in itself questionable, and it is obvious that the social milieu, health status, and other variables of the environment have a profound effect upon an individual's capacity to realize his psychological potential, whatever its genetic basis may be. It appears to many anthropologists today that gene action has no direct influence upon the behavior of individuals or upon "national character." But the field of behavioral genetics is still in its infancy and its discoveries will have important implications for students of human variation. All we can conclude at present is that cultural conditioning rather than genes is the critical factor in performance level on I.Q. tests. For this reason, anthropologists have been quick to counter the claims of Arthur R. Jensen (1923-), a psychologist, and William B. Shockley (1910-), a physicist, that I.Q. scores and genetic constitutions are demonstrably correlated. However, with regard to certain psychological abnormalities there is a genetic basis for variation, just as there is for inherited expressions in somatic diseases. Conditions such as vitamin B deficiency and debilitation brought on by enzymatic malfunctions are known to have mental affects. But these conditions, of which some are correctable by medical attention, are not related to the issues Jensen and Shockley discuss.

RACIAL PALEONTOLOGY

Anatomically modern man—*Homo sapiens*—makes his debut in the fossil record in deposits dating to about forty thousand years ago. Our most ancient representative found thus far is a skull from Niah Cave in Borneo, but Cro-Magnon-type men were living in Europe some thirty thousand years ago, thus indicating that mankind as we know it was widely distributed over much of the world during the final part of the Pleistocene. Bands of *Homo sapiens* had migrated to the American and Australian continents by twenty-five thousand years ago. Preceding our own species were other kinds of hominids, which have been assigned different taxonomic names on the basis of their distinguishing morphological characters, particularly of the skull. In Europe the antecedent population has been called Neanderthal and was assigned to its own species in the last century. Today most anthropologists would regard this hominid of forty thousand to one-hundred-twenty-five thousand years ago as *Homo sapiens,* although not like any member of our species living now. In Africa and Asia collaterals of Neanderthals have been found too, but their taxonomic status is uncertain. In all probability they, along with Neanderthal man of Europe and anatomically modern men, have a common ancestor in the Middle Pleistocene population called *Homo erectus* (formerly *Pithecanthropus*). Bones of this hominid who lived a half-million years ago have been found in deposits in Europe, Africa, and Asia. Ultimate human origins are still unclear, but we know from the fossil record that a creature who moved bipedally, had reduced canine teeth, and possibly made stone tools was living in Africa some four million years ago. This hominid has been given the genus name *Australopithecus.* Some anthropologists would push back the origins of man to fifteen million years on the basis of some fossil jaws and teeth recovered from Africa and India. *Ramapithecus,* as the protohominid has been called, may have evolved from groups of fossil apes whose remains date to still earlier times. But in 1856 when the first Neanderthal specimen was found, this picture of human evolution was still unknown.

It appeared to most early students of fossil man that no very great temporal hiatus separated Neanderthals and Cro-Magnon *Homo sapiens* from one another or both from contemporary populations. For lack of accurate dating methods, a relative chronology was established for prehistoric specimens associated with the remains of extinct animals and with archeological artifacts for which relative temporal sequences were being arranged. Using a limited number of cranial features as criteria for reconstructing racial lines, the fossils from Chancelade in France were classified as prehistoric Eskimos. Today we know that the population from this site existed some seventeen thousand years ago! At Combe Capelle, also in France and known to have been inhabited at least thirty-four thousand years ago, skeletons were found that were called the earliest ancestors of the Mediterranean race. There were analagous efforts to demonstrate that the historic inhabitants of the Canary Islands, the Guanchos, were Cro-Magnon survivals, while skeletons from the Grimaldi caves along the Monaco-Italian Riviera were identified as Negroids. These latter two populations have been given an antiquity of twenty thousand to thirty thousand years before the present.

So long as the hominid fossil record included a very few specimens, every find was thought to represent a universal stage or grade through which mankind had passed. Huxley was the first writer to include the fossil finds of prehistoric man, such as were known in the 1860s, in a phylogenetic tree. Huxley described man's emergence from an ancient apeline, for which no fossil representative had been found at that time, but out of this arose a hypothetical ape-man, then Neanderthals, and finally early *sapiens* of anatomically modern aspect. From these latter populations came the races of man living today. This interpretation of human phylogeny is called the *unilinear* theory. When represented by a diagram, it is easily recognizable by its palm tree shape, the foliage at the apex of the tree indicating the recent raciation of our species. This theory, which has followers today, does not exclude the possibility that raciation occurred in the lines of Neanderthals and their antecedents, but modern races are all represented in relation to the emergence of *Homo sapiens* some forty thousand years ago when our species appears to have begun its adaptive radiation. Neanderthal man is put in the direct line of *sapiens* descent, for in this phylogenetic theory all fossil hominids are included in a single evolutionary series.[21]

The earliest phylogenetic trees for man to be published were prepared by Haeckel in 1868 to illustrate his polygenetic theory of racial evolution.[22] He classified the species into two major racial groups on the basis of differences in hair form. Both lines originated from a common ape-man ancestor to which he gave the name later assigned to the find in Java in 1891. Haeckel's theory was taken up by later anthropologists who applied it to their thesis of human raciation, which bears the name of the *polyphyletic* school. These anthropologists argue that the races of man have a great antiquity. Each contemporary race is given its complement of fossil progenitors according to the geographical localities in which both occur. Thus the fossil find called Rhodesian man from Zambia is placed in the ancestral line of living populations of southern Africa. In the same way, the fossil men from Java are placed along the racial pedigree of contemporary populations living in Southeast Asia, Australia, and Melanesia. The fossils are also classified into evolutionary grades that more or less correspond to geological divisions of the prehistoric time scale. For example, a Neanderthal grade includes fossils from Europe, Africa, and Asia that can be dated to the period of around one hundred twenty-five thousand to forty thousand years ago. They are preceded by Middle Pleistocene fossils of *Homo erectus* grade from the same continental areas. Only in the earlier part of the Pleistocene is a common ancestor found—*Australopithecus*. The tree diagram of the poly-

21. C. Loring Brace, "The Fate of the *'Classic'* Neanderthals: a Consideration of Hominid Catastrophism," *Current Anthropology* 5 (1964):3-34.

22. E. Ray Lankester, trans., *The History of Creation: or the Development of the Earth and Its Inhabitants by the Action of Natural Causes, Etc. by Ernst Heinrich Haeckel* (New York: D. Appleton, 1868), pp. 263-277, 325-333.

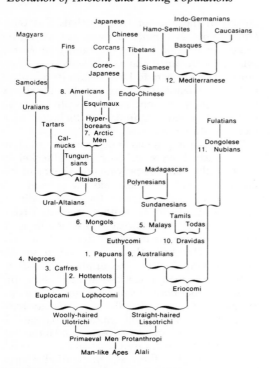

FIGURE 4.4. Pedigree of the Twelve Species of Men according to Ernst Haeckel's phylogenetic tree of 1876. From E. Ray Lankester, trans. **The History of Creation, or the Development of the Earth and Its Inhabitants by the Action of Natural Causes, etc.** 4th edition. New York: D. Appleton, 1907, vol. 2, p. 417.

phyletic theory looks like a cactus with its stems moving upward in parallel fashion. While this does not resemble Haeckel's tree in detail, its statement is sufficiently close to the tenets of polygenesis to be obvious. Twentieth-century anthropologists who have favored this interpretation of human evolution and raciation include Franz Weidenreich (1873-1948)[23] and Coon.[24] In reply to the question of how all men can belong to a single species today given separate but parallel evolutionary lines, Weidenreich and Coon have answered that reproductive isolation never became so complete as to provide the opportunity for speciation to have taken place.

Other types of phylogenetic trees have been designed that represent theories of human

descent from which Neanderthals are excluded from the line leading to *sap:ens*. Supporters of the *presapiens* theory would exclude *Homo erectus* as well from our ancestry, maintaining that *Homo sapiens* is of much greater antiquity that the forty millenia commonly ascribed to sapient origins. The earliest evolutionary line of *sapiens* was separate from those of other kinds of hominids who lived as contemporaries for many thousands of years but had become extinct by the time Cro-Magnon appeared upon the scene. There are fewer enthusiasts for *presapiens* theory today than there were at the turn of the century, but the existence of a handful of fossil skulls of uncertain taxonomy has served to keep the idea alive.[25] The possibility that the genus *Homo* may have to be assigned to certain fossil specimens from Africa that represent populations contemporary with *Australopithecus* is another issue, but both this hypothesis and the tenets of the presapiens school bear many elements of the venerable theory of monogenesis. Today there is general acceptance for the *pre-Neanderthal* theory that maintains that the ancestors of both Neanderthals and early representatives of modern man formed a single population at the end of the Middle Pleistocene, but by forty thousand years ago the Neanderthal line had become extinct and men of modern aspect were replacing them in many parts of the Old World.[26]

As human paleontologists and archeologists were reconstructing the broad picture of man's biological evolution and cultural development, reactions against the nineteenth-century notion of psychic unity and the use of the comparative method were set into motion by a group of anthropologists who came to be called *diffusionists*. These scholars denied that there was any sound evidence to prove the existence of universal cultural stages from primi-

23. Franz Weidenreich, *Apes, Giants and Men* (Chicago: University of Chicago, 1946).

24. Carleton S. Coon, *The Origin of Races.*

25. Henri V. Vallois, "The Origin of *Homo sapiens,*" *Ideas on Human Evolution: Selected Essays, 1949-1961,* ed. William W. Howells (Cambridge: Harvard University, 1962), pp. 473-499.

26. Wilfred E. Le Gros Clark, "Bones of Contention," *Journal of the Royal Anthropological Institute* 88 (1958):131-145.

tive to civilized lifeways that Europeans had passed through, but along whose course peoples of other continents were survivals of arrested evolutionary growth. Rather, they held the view that man was fundamentally an uninventive creature, major cultural innovations having been made only once or twice in human history. From a center of origin, culture traits were diffused by imitation into marginal areas, or else culture-bearers migrated to far-flung parts of the world bringing with them a baggage of material products and belief systems from their homeland. Both diffusion and migration were thought to be primary mechanisms of culture history. Among these diffusionists was the German philologist Friedrich Max Müller (1823-1900) who traced all European folktales to Sanskrit sources from Central and South Asia.[27] His compatriot, the archeologist Hugo Winckler (1863-1913), had a pan-Babylonian diffusionist theory that had

27. Friedrich Max Müller, *Lectures on the Science of Language* (London: Charles Scribner, 1862).

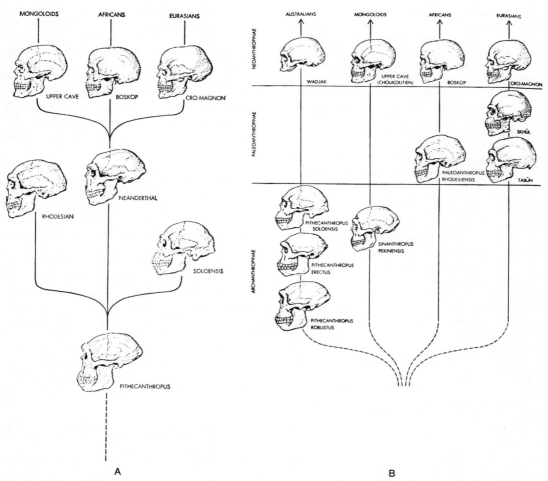

FIGURE 4.5. Phylogenetic trees representing the (A) unilinear school and the (B) polyphyletic school. From William W. Howells, "The Distribution of Man." **Scientific American** 203 (1960): 118 and 120.

great popularity.[28] The British anatomist Sir Grafton Elliot Smith (1871-1937) believed that all cultural innovations were derived ultimately from ancient Egypt.[29]

Smith's more moderate colleagues were prepared to consider the existence of several centers of cultural invention over the span of human history, and this became the major thesis of the German *Kulturkreis* (culture-circle) school. Emphasis upon regular movements of people from centers of cultural innovation was made by Fritz Graebner (1877-1934), one of the founders of this theory. He taught that early man had invented the fundamental elements of culture, but then migrating bands of people became isolated from one another. In due course, each band developed its unique way of life, which Graebner called the *primitive culture*. As these bands settled over the continents, further cultural changes occurred. It was the task of the anthropologist to reconstruct these tribal histories. To do this successfully, the specialist of the Kulturkreis school needed all the help he could get from the research of colleagues in archeology, linguistics, and anthropology. Biological considerations of race became an important element of this approach.[30] Meanwhile, American anthropologists were emphasizing the role of diffusion rather than migration, an orientation that gave rise to the *culture area* concept that has characterized the historical approach to the study of culture in his country.

It is not surprising that these nonbiological theories of transmission of ideas and mass movements of populations became models for the interpretations of racial histories. Easily absorbed into the culturally oriented theories of antiquarians, folklorists, historians, and comparative philologists were the racial classifications and diagrams of ancestral stems and population affinities. With the increase in prehistoric skeletal data, racial paleontology became a popular endeavor that complemented these other methods. Racial trees were drawn by cultural historians as well as by students of man's biological variations. It was common practice to treat one or a few physical similarities in different populations as evidence of ancestral affinity, a procedure that persisted well after the date of the discovery of Mendelian genetics. Thus the tribal

Ainu of Japan were called Far Eastern Europeans on the basis of their hirsute bodies and light skin color. Those populations of small body size living in tropical Africa, the Andaman Islands, Malaya, the Philippines, and New Guinea were lumped together as an ancient pygmy race that had been widely distributed throughout much of the world in earlier times.

According to the English anthropologist Alfred Cort Haddon (1855-1914), movements of people were determined by two factors: (1) a driving force, such as expulsion of one group by another from one habitat into a new one on account of dearth of food, essential resources, overpopulation, or oppression by an enemy, and (2) a control or inducement which provides direction to migrations. Environmental pressure of climate and geological changes were not excluded as other causitive factors. An excerpt from Haddon's *The Wanderings of Peoples,* published in 1911, will illustrate the idiom of many writings of this genre. In describing the racial history of South Asia he says

the greater part of Iran was originally inhabited by the broad-headed Alpines, who are still represented by the Tajiks, but in Susiana there was in ancient times—and traces still persist—a low-typed dark race, which is usually regarded as allied to the Pre-Dravidian stock of south India, or which may have been of true Negroid stock. From the Eur-Asians steppes came Proto-Nordics, who became known to history as Medes and Persians, but Semitic migrations have modified the type of the latter as did incursions of tribes allied to the Turki. Some authorities, such as Ripley, see in the dark, dolichocephalic Persians, especially the Lori, a strong Mediterranean strain, while the Farsi are relatively blond dolichocephals, the 'Aryans' of many authors. So far

28. James Alexander Craig, trans. and ed., *The History of Babylon and Assyria by Hugo Winckler* (New York: Charles Scribner's Sons, 1907).

29. Grafton Elliot Smith, *The Ancient Egyptians and Their Influences upon Civilization in Europe* (London: Harper and Brothers, 1911).

30. Fritz Graebner, *Methode der Ethnologie* (Heidelberg: Carl Winter's, 1911).

as is known the bulk of the population of India has been stationary. The oldest existing stratum is that represented by various Pre-Dravidian jungle tribes. The Dravidians may have been always in India. . . . The Munda-speaking peoples (Munda, Bhumji, Ho, etc.) are stated to resemble so closely the Dravidians as to be indistinguishable from them. They appear to have been the original inhabitants of the valley of the Ganges in western Bengal; after many wanderings, apparently across India, they settled mainly in Chutia Nagpur. . . The first migration into India of which we have evidence is that of Aryan-speaking peoples, perhaps early in the second millenium B.C. . . There is a strongly marked brachycephalic element in the population of western India. Risley believes this is a result of so-called Scythian invasions. . . The foreign element is certainly Alpine, not Mongolian, and it may be due to a migration of which the history has been unwritten.[31]

Descriptions of this sort that uncritically pull together data and theories that may not be directly pertinent to the main question of human variation and its evolution do not mean that the goal of determining population affinities is without value or beyond the reach of scientific methodology. It is obvious that all contemporary populations of man are derived from earlier ones. Nor can migrations of populations be discounted when we consider such impressive invasions as the movements of Gothic peoples in Europe from the third to sixth centuries A.D. and the invasions of the Ottoman Turks of the seventeenth to twentieth centuries. From 1600 to 1950 over sixty-five million people migrated from Europe to the Americas. However, many movements of people have taken place as continuous displacements of families and small groups and not as migrations of entire nations, as was the case with the Golden Horde of Genghis Khan in the thirteenth century. We shall examine some other limitations to the traditional approach to racial paleontology in a moment, but this would be a good place to review some of the modern interpretations of human diversity in prehistoric times that are based upon paleontological data.

HUMAN VARIABILITY SINCE THE PLEISTOCENE

As the Ice Age glaciers of Europe were retreating northwards some twelve thousand years ago, the Cro-Magnon-like populations were replaced by other groups of *sapiens* who adapted to the climatic change to warmer temperatures. Their settlements were situated along seacoasts and river banks rather than in the cave shelters preferred by earlier inhabitants of their hunting grounds. Stone tool industries developed in post-Pleistocene times that were distinctive from those of earlier times. The term *Mesolithic* (Middle Stone Age) has been given to these artifacts to distinguish them from earlier tool-making traditions of the *Paleolithic* (Old Stone Age). Mesolithic peoples in the Near East began experimenting with plant cultivation as early as the seventh millenium B.C. The shift from a hunting-gathering economy to a food-producing economy with garden crops, domesticated animals, and sedentary communities living in villages marks a cultural development called the *Neolithic* (New Stone Age). It was during this time in the Near East that pottery and weaving emerged as important crafts, and one of its technological hallmarks is the polished stone axe. Neolithic traditions were firmly established in the Nile Valley before 4000 B.C. and in western Europe a thousand years later. Now we enter the dawn of the period of recorded history in this part of the world. With the invention of writing came the development of metalurgy, bronze coming into use by 3500 B.C. in the Near East. Iron was used as a raw material by 1900 B.C. among the Hittites whose secret of smelting the metal remained their monopoly until the dissolution of the Hittite empire 500 years later. The Roman invasions of Gaul commenced during the European Iron Age of the first millenium B.C.

This sequence of economic and technological events in Europe and western Asia is reflected in areas of North Africa and South Asia, but is less obvious in the cultural developments of sub-Saharan Africa and the Far East. Cultural attainments in these regions

31. Alfred Cort Haddon, *The Wanderings of Peoples* (Cambridge: Cambridge University, 1927), pp. 25-27.

have different histories. The cultural history of the Americas was distinctive from the time those continents were entered by Paleolithic hunters from northeastern Asia. Agriculture was invented independently in the New World. Oceania and Australia saw still other cultural patterns, food-production being unknown in the southern continent until the arrival of Europeans. By the fourth century A.D. Easter Island, the farthest island of the Polynesian triangle of settlement from New Zealand to Hawaii and 1200 miles from the nearest inhabited land, was settled by seafarers populating the vast area of the Pacific Ocean, perhaps the last frontier of human settlement until historic times.

Skeletal series from sites of terminal Pleistocene and early post-Pleistocene antiquity are more abundant and contain greater numbers of individuals than do series taken from more ancient desposits. In certain cases, the anthropologist may be able to describe what are called *cemetery populations,* although specimens collected from a specific deposit may not represent portions of true breeding populations in an evolutionary sense. In addition to the anatomical features of ancient human remains, the student of skeletal biology is interested in reconstructing the demographic character of an extinct population (i.e., its patterns of mortality and morbidity, fertility and fecundity, growth and development, population density, health and nutritional status, and the diseases most prevalent). From these data and from the use of anthropometric and statistical procedures, the anthropologist attempts to discover how human populations have undergone microevolutionary changes over time.

In Europe the earliest discoveries of Mesolithic human remains were made in Sweden in 1843 at a site called Stangenäs, but the significance of the skeletons was not appreciated until many years later. In 1865 mounds of sea shells at Muge, Portugal, yielded skeletons of similar age. Ofnet Cave in Bavaria was excavated in 1907-1908 and from it some thirty-four skulls were removed. Ten burials were taken from Téviec, an island off the coast of Brittany, in the late 1920s. Other important Mesolithic sites have been located in France, Germany, the Low Countries, and in many places in eastern Europe.

Anthropologists describing these specimens have noted morphological features that distinguish them from the Pleistocene populations of Europe, especially with respect to their cranial anatomy. The Ofnet series contains some individuals with broad cranial vaults, the earliest indication of this trend toward brachycephalization in this part of the world. This same feature appears in lower frequency in skeletal remains from Mugem and Téviec. Most Mesolithic people of Europe were of shorter stature than Cro-Magnon-like populations preceding them. While earlier anthropologists assigned racial names to these skeletal series and sought to relate them to living populations, it is not until we examine skeletons of those Neolithic peoples who came into Europe from the Near East that we can find in the skeletal record any anatomical evidence that we are looking at probable forebears of historic European populations. However, so great is the variability of Neolithic, Bronze Age, and Iron Age skeletons that we can use the term *European* only in a very general sense in the identification of these earlier populations. We know that some groups like the *Beaker* folk, manufacturers of characteristic clay vessels with incised decorations, were distributed over a geographical range from the Balkans to England during the period of 1000-2000 B.C. They buried their dead in round earth barrows, sometimes placing cremated remains in urns under these mounds. From what is recoverable of their skeletons we know that their heads were large and broad, their faces and noses quite narrow. These features still occur in high frequency in portions of southeastern Europe, but we are really uncertain who their closest living relatives might be. Another group of ancient people with distinctive anatomical features is associated with archeological artifacts of the so-called *Battle Axe* culture. They lived in northern Europe, contemporaries of the Beaker people to the south. Population affinities with contemporary Europeans can be made with greater confidence in series from the Iron Age, but with the rise of Roman rule a few centuries before the birth of Christ Europe experienced profound demographic changes that were unparalled until the time of the Industrial Revolution.

The origins of those Neolithic populations who invaded Mesolithic Europe remain unknown, although the Near East seems a likely center for this migration on the basis of both anatomical and archeological evidence. However, the Mesolithic people living in the Mount Carmel region of Israel about 8000 B.C. seem biologically unlike prehistoric and modern peoples of Europe. The *Natufians,* as they are called, were of robust body build, dolichocranic, with relatively broad noses, and moderately broad faces. By 6000 B.C. their hunting territories were occupied by different populations who practiced stock-breeding and agriculture and whose skeletal anatomy more nearly resembles that of peoples presently inhabiting portions of the Mediterranean basin. Skeletons from Egyptian and Mesopotamian tombs of the Bronze Age also seem more like Europeans now inhabiting the shorelines of the Mediterranean Sea. For reasons still unclear, a trend towards brachycrany begins in the Near East after 2000 B.C. Populations to be seen today in Turkey, Macedonia, and Greece are not represented in high frequency in the cemetery populations of these areas until after the tenth century A.D. Mesolithic populations of North Africa show a high frequency of skeletal similarities to the Neolithic peoples of the northern and eastern shores of the Mediterranean. Around 6500 B.C. the site of el-Mekta was occupied by people with the short stature, narrow cranial vault, and long face found from this Mesolithic period until today among Berber tribes and other native peoples of Algeria, Tunisia, and Morocco.

Present-day Bushmen people live in inhospitable areas of the Kalihari desert in southwestern Africa. This is not their ancient homeland, and historic sources of the seventeenth century A.D. indicate that the southward thrust of Bantu-speaking peoples forced these hunters into the relict region where they survive in small numbers now. For many years anthropologists thought that the Bushmen, or populations related to them, extended across tremendous portions of the African continent, perhaps even as far north as the Sudanese Nile. It was in this area at a place called Singa that a skull was found in a late or terminal

Pleistocene context. This specimen has many of the anatomical features of modern Bushmen skulls. Similarly puzzling finds were made at the Homa Shell Mound in Kenya and in the Transvaal region of South Africa. The Boskop skeletal material from this latter region has been called *Bushmanoid,* and its antiquity may be terminal Pleistocene. Bambandyanolo and Mapungubue are sites that have been dated to 1000-1400 A.D., which is the period of iron-using in southern Africa, and their skeletal remains show many anatomical similarities to living Bushmen living far to the south. It is primarily with respect to their short stature that living Bushmen differ from these possible genetically related forebears. Closely related to Bushmen are the other contemporary populations called Hottentots and Strandlopers, groups that are taller and skeletally more robust.

We have been less fortunate in recovering a skeletal record for those agricultural and herding populations who replaced Bushman groups over parts of Africa. The Zulu Wars of the nineteenth century were the final push of sub-Saharan Bantu-speaking people into southern Africa where they came in contact with colonizing Europeans. But the prehistoric representatives of these invaders remain unknown. For many years it was thought that some human remains of uncertain antiquity from Asselar near Timbuktu in the Sahara were evidence of early *Negroids.* Skeletal remains, which are better candidates for the macropopulation of Africa today, have been found in late Mesolithic deposits at Kourounkorokale and Khartum in the Sudan. These are dated to about 3250 B.C. Mesolithic sites of Gamble's Cave, Vaivasha, and Elmenteita, all in Kenya, have yielded skeletons that possess a number of anatomical similarities to North African Mesolithic populations who lived along the shores of the Mediterranean. They do not appear to be ancestral to the modern populations of Ethiopia and the Sudan.

Prehistoric skeletons of pygmies have not been found in Africa. Historical data indicate that as late as the sixteenth century hunting bands of pygmies were distributed along the western coast of Africa as far north as Liberia, while they extended inland to the shores of Lake Albert. Modern pygmies are found in a much narrower geographical range, but they have continued to practice a hunting-gathering economy in areas adjacent to the settlements of agricultural peoples. Gene flow between these communities is one-way: from the pygmy into the village populations. For this reason a high frequency of pygmy genes occurs in the taller populations. There is no reason to support a thesis of a pan-pygmy migration in ancient times from Africa to those parts of Asia where small-statured hunters and gathers still survive in remote enclaves. No skeletal remains of pygmies are known from Asia with possible exceptions in Laos and in the Philippines. It has been suggested that short stature may have survival value under particular conditions of the forest environment when subsistence depends in large part upon success in tracking and hunting. The same explanation would not apply to short Bushmen, but their stature is somewhat greater than that of pygmy populations as the latter have been defined by anthropologists. It is possible that pygmy body size was acquired independently in the different parts of the world where these populations are now found, their ancestors being of taller stature.

What may be a Neanderthal cranial fragment has been found at a thirty thousand year old site in Afghanistan, but South Asia has been slow in yielding human skeletal remains for the period between the adaptive radiation of *Ramapithecus* and the dawn of the Mesolithic horizon. In the Indian subcontinent the Mesolithic is called the *Late Stone Age,* and from its deposits we find human skeletal remains. The earliest dated Late Stone Age deposit is at Sarai Nahar Rai near Allahabad, which is given an antiquity of some ten thousand years. The prehistoric inhabitants of the island of Sri Lanka (Ceylon) off the southern tip of India are known from skeletons dating to about 6000 B.C. These are from the river site of Bellanbandi Palassa, and the prehistoric population has been given the nontaxonomic name of the *Balangodese.* These ancient people have many anatomical similarities in skeletal features to the tribal hunting people of the island, the Veddas, who are descendants of aboriginal people encountered by invaders from the mainland around the fifth century B.C. Other Late Stone Age sites in South Asia date to the

second and third millenia B.C. by which time the Bronze Age culture of the Indus Valley Civilization was already a going concern in the area defined today by the political divisions of Pakistan, the Panjab, Gujarat, and even to the headwaters of the Ganges.

The largest skeletal series from prehistoric South Asia comes from the cemeteries at Harappa, but smaller series are known from other sites within the sphere of influence of the Indus Civilization. The development of agriculture and animal domestication in this part of the world derived from Neolithic cultures of the Near East, but in southern India the rise of a Neolithic lifeway may be traceable to influences from Southeast Asia via Burma and Assam beginning around 2000 B.C. In eastern India the Iron Age was flourishing around 350 B.C., but to the north the precious metal was being used by 1100 B.C.

Superimposed upon paleontological and archeological efforts to reconstruct a picture of prehistoric South Asia is the sacred tradition of the Aryan invasion that is supposed to have taken place in several waves by 1500 B.C. Whatever linguists have to tell us about the antiquity of Indo-European languages in this part of the world, skeletal evidence of Aryans, whoever they may have been, is lacking. At least we have no certain way of recognizing an Aryan, be he alive or dead (i.e., as a skeletal specimen). If Aryan bones have been recovered, they go unrecognized. Yet this legendary history of Aryan influence, so apparent in the speech and religion of many South Asians, remains a dominant theme in the minds of many prehistorians.

The results of an anatomical analysis of all skeletal series from South Asia have not yet been published, but preliminary data from measurements of genetic distance indicate that the phenotypic patterns observed in the prehistoric specimens are not markedly different from what the anthropologist finds in his study of modern populations in this part of Asia. Indeed, the establishment of good biological continua along the lines of the Balangodese-Vedda study are very promising in analysis of South Asian skeletal data thus far. Claims of pygmy populations in India are founded upon very tenuous evidence, namely the incidence of spiral hair form in very low frequency among short-statured and dark-skinned tribal populations of Kerela. It is more likely that these features are the result of some African genetic material entering India when slave ships found harbor along the western coast of India. It is known that slaves would escape from these ships from time to time and seek asylum in the interior. It is also conceivable that spiral hair form among these tribes is due to a mutated gene.

Eastern Asia has a rich fossil record of Pleistocene hominids. At Choukoutien near Peking, from whence *Homo erectus* (*Sinanthropus*) specimens were found, a locality called the Upper Cave has yielded a small series of skeletons dated to early post-Pleistocene times. These specimens are interesting because they possess a broad range of anatomical differences from one another. One investigator described the specimen as a male of *Proto-Ainu* stock with two wives, one a *Melanesian* and the other an *Eskimo!* Without resorting to a racial classification of such absurdity, we can appreciate that the Upper Cave specimens may reveal the existence of several different populations occupying northeastern Asia during this period. From such diversified populations, if such existed, may have come those ancestors of native Americans who continued their migrations into the New World when the Bering Strait was still locked in ice.

At Djalai-Nor in Manchuria, a pre-Neolithic site excavated by the Japanese during their occupation of northern China just before World War II, were found two human skulls that reveal a number of anatomical features found in high incidence today among Manchurians. Cemeteries that can be properly labeled Chinese, although of Neolithic antiquity, are known. These graves were filled long before the beginnings of a literary and historic period in China around 3000 B.C. There has been a continuous movement of populations from the Far East into southern China and Southeast Asia beginning as early as late Pleistocene times. A westward extension of Chinese people into Tibet and Nepal occurred somewhat later in the historic period of the Buddhist chronicles. There are no recognized skeletal remains of great age for the Ainu, the probable aborigines of Japan. But skeletons of

the Jamon period of about 7500 B.C. have been found. These specimens and those from the fourth century A.D. resemble in skeletal anatomy the contemporary peoples of Japan.

Well before the invasions of northern Chinese populations into the mainland and island sectors of Southeast Asia, the predominant population in this region was marked by a robust cranial architecture that led some anthropologists to conclude that here must be the direct descendants of *Homo erectus* or of an evolutionary grade called *Neanderthaloid*. Labels of this sort do not carry us far and are as appropriate as calling Neanderthals of France *European Javanese!* What is obvious is that the descendants of the cranially robust people of the late Pleistocene site of Ngandong and the early post-Pleistocene site of Wadjak, both in Java, are probably represented in some of the gene pools of Southeast Asia, Australia, and Melanesia today. At a terminal Pleistocene site called Aitape in New Guinea some skeletal remains have been found that may indicate that *Homo erectus* had survived on the island longer than elsewhere. By forty thousand years ago *Homo sapiens* was living in Southeast Asia, as the Niah Cave skull from Borneo has demonstrated.

About ten thousand years ago, Mesolithic peoples migrated into this part of the world, coming perhaps from northern Asia. These nomadic hunters were succeeded by Neolithic populations coming from the same source. Dutch scholars have observed that certain tribal populations on the mainland and islands have anatomical characters that suggest that they were less directly influenced by these new arrivals of earlier times. Rather, these isolated groups share a number of anatomical features with the contemporary populations of Australia and Melanesia where the northern Asiatic phenotypic pattern is not obvious. In the earlier anthropological literature this more robust and apparently more ancient phenotypic pattern was labeled *Australoid*. A revival of this term is not recommended, but it seems reasonable to conclude that there has been the continuation of a pre-Mesolithic genetic element in certain portions of Southeast Asia and points east.

It was probably from Southeast Asia that Oceania was settled, first by Melanesian seafarers and later by peoples from Micronesia and Polynesia. The settlement of some islands within the Polynesian triangle continued as late as 1850 when it was brought to an end by European intervention. Outside of New Guinea and the Philippines, there is little evidence to suggest a Pleistocene occupation of the Pacific area by human groups.

Both North and South America have provided a skeletal record of some antiquity, the archeological evidence indicating that the common estimate of twenty-five thousand years ago for the settlement of these continents by man may turn out to be too conservative. However, skeletal remains found thus far on these continents are not of such a profound age. The Guitarrero Cave mandible from Peru has been dated to 9000 to 10,000 B.C., and other claims of early man in the New World are either based upon uncertain dating results or are somewhat more recent.

The fallacy of tracing lines of descent for contemporary populations backward into the Pleistocene and calling forth some grizzled fossil skull as an honored ancestor is more obvious to us today than it was to racial anthropologists of the earlier part of this century. In the first place, we now recognize that evolutionary forces have been operating continuously upon all populations that have existed from the Pleistocene to the present, but without a complete skeletal record of all intermediate populations the extremes of any biological continuum must exhibit more differences than similarities. Secondly, traits considered as distinctive markers of an ancestral line could be the results of parallel evolution in separate populations rather than signs of affinity. Finally, for the reason that the same evolutionary mechanisms were operating in the remote past as are now affecting our species, it is apparent that any attempt to classify fossil skeletal series into narrow ancestral lines associated with particular modern populations is defied by the very nature of these phylogenetic histories themselves. Therefore we are forced to conclude that beyond the span of a few centuries all such lines become tenuous, and within the scope of millenia affinities may be unrecognizable and consequently untraceable.[32]

MEASUREMENT OF GENETIC DISTANCES IN POPULATIONS

Recognition of the hazards of racial paleontology has meant the fall of many a phylogenetic tree that had its roots in the Pleistocene and its upper branches in the clouds of typological theory. But given the problems involved in tracing biological continua beyond the scope of a few thousand years, what might be learned of the affinities of prehistoric populations from a study of degrees of genetic distance between populations existing today? With new and sophisticated statistical procedures and the indispensable convenience of computers, modern anthropologists have looked at the enduring problems of human phylogeny and genetic distance in a way that was unheard of a generation ago.

The use of gene frequency counts derived from phenotypic trait frequencies has allowed for more accurate comparisons of contemporary populations and facilitated statistical calculations that developed along with the growth of the field of genetics. Pearson's *Coefficient of Racial Likeness* was one early biometric effort to combine anthropometric data from measurements of different physical characters into a single value that would then be used to measure general divergence between the various populations represented in the sample. Distance statistics, which replaced Pearson's formula, were the *Generalized Distance, or D^2* statistic of Mahalanobis, and the *Shape* statistics of Penrose which measure *multivariate distances*. More recently, multivariate analysis and *discriminate function analysis* have been most widely used. Research carried out between 1967 and 1972 under the auspices of the Human Adaptability Section of the International Biological Program (IBP) has been published by the IBP and is reported as well in a symposium volume entitled *The Assessment of Population Affinities in Man.*

32. Jean Hiernaux, "The Concept of Race and Taxonomy in Mankind," *The Concept of Race*. M. F. Ashley Montagu, ed. (New York: Free Press, 1964), pp. 29-45 and Francis E. Johnston, "Racial Taxonomies from an Evolutionary Perspective," *American Anthropologist* 66 (1964):822-827.

This will remain for sometime text for students involved in research on genetic distance.[33]

By avoiding the biases and limitations of previously employed statistical methods for establishing population affinities, modern researchers can better demonstrate actual genetic relationships, the ramification of one or more groups from a parental population, and the splitting of a segment of a macropopulation. Two-way gene flow patterns of a segment from a macropopulation are also assessed with contemporary methods. And populations relatively free from effects of gene migration and drift may be more easily recognizable as biological continua wherein major changes have come about through differential rates of mutation and specific targets of natural selection. Two examples of recent research projects in this area will be helpful.

A few years ago two biometric statisticians selected fifteen populations from different geographical areas and determined the degrees of divergence between them. This project was carried out using a number of anthropometric characters and frequencies of genes of various blood group systems. Separate phylogenetic trees were drawn up based on these two kinds of data collected. The patterns of affinity were quite similar for the anthropometric and serological results, neither diverging significantly from classifications of the populations that had been obtained by nonstatistical or different statistical methods. However, the phylogenetic trees that were drawn up with these data were not free from biases. The selection of the measurements and gene frequencies are not representative of the degree of variability present in the populations under consideration. Furthermore, results may be interpreted according to long established notions of affinity. For example, no one would imagine that Pawnee Indians and the Tasaday of the Philippines would show the same kinds of distance values that could be expected from studies of Hungarian Jews and Polish Jews or, for that matter, between Polish Jews and non-Jewish people in Poland. The fact that equal weight is accorded all characters in many kinds of genetic distance studies is itself a reason for caution in accepting some estimates, such as the sort we have described above. Certainly some traits are more important in an evolutionary and phylogenetic sense than are others.

Another recent study was based upon data for fifty-eight single genes. The contemporary population included in the sample was taken from widely separated geographical areas. The lapse of time since their presumed separation from a parental *Homo sapiens* stock was assumed to be of the order of from ten thousand to forty thousand years. For populations whose ancestors settled in America, Australia, and Melanesia, migrations would have commenced in the Pleistocene. The tree diagram that developed from this statistical analysis of genetic data showed the Lapps of northern Scandinavia sharing more genetic correspondences with other Europeans than with the Asiatic populations with which they have been associated by earlier racial anthropologists. The Ainu appeared to be genetically similar to their Oriental neighbors and not close to Europeans after all, hairy bodies, beards, and light skin colors aside. Another feature of the phylogenetic tree in this project is the appearance of three main branches giving rise to Africans, Europeans, and Orientals, the latter branch including Oceanians and native Americans. Europeans showed intermediate status in degree of genetic distance to the other two groups. This is explained by the researchers as an indication that modern Europeans are descendants from Neolithic farmers living in the Near East some nine thousand years ago, a people who were themselves genetically intermediate between Africans and Asians. Once these Neolithic invaders settled in Europe, they mixed with the Mesolithic populations already there, and gave rise to European populations as we recognize them today. Convincing as these conclusions might seem, they suffer from two serious limitations that arise from the use of single gene data: (1) the problem of establishing rates of genetic change, and (2) the arbitrary practice of using certain genes and not others. Nevertheless the researchers who carried out this study believe that their phylogenetic trees are more accurately rendered than those based upon an-

33. Joseph S. Weiner and Johan Huizinga, eds., *The Assessment of Population Affinities in Man* (Oxford: Clarendon, 1972).

thropometric data. They question the use of polygenic characters as providing good indicators of population affinity since the variables of stature, cranial form, skin pigmentation and the like are subject to short-term environmental effects, hence are too unstable for use in genetic-distance studies.[34] This may be true, but thus far we have no well-documented case of a human skeleton extending his arm for the taking of a blood sample or opening his jaws voluntarily for submission to a PTC taste-sensitivity determination. With our colleagues in vertebrate paleontology facing an assemblage of dinosaur bones, we must make our phylogenetic statements on the basis of the data at hand. But our statements about skeletal biology may come closer to reconstructing what really happened with populations in the past if supplemented by data of

genetic-distance measurements derived from the study of biological variations is contemporary populations.

For Further Reading

Avers, Charlotte J. *Evolution.* New York: Harper & Row. 1974. This is a concise and readable survey of evolutionary theory with an interesting section on man's biological history.

Baker, Paul T. and Weiner, Joseph S., eds. *The Biology of Human Adaptability.* Oxford: Clarendon, 1966. Population genetics and man's

34. Luigi Luca Cavalli-Sforza, "The Genetics of Human Populations," *Scientific American* 231 (1974): 80-89 and Luigi Luca Cavalli-Sforza and W. F. Bodmer, *The Genetics of Human Populations* (San Francisco: W. H. Freeman, 1971).

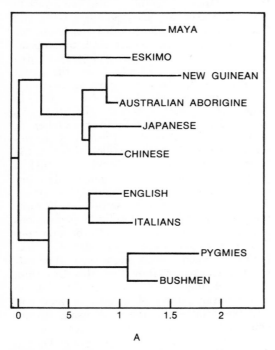

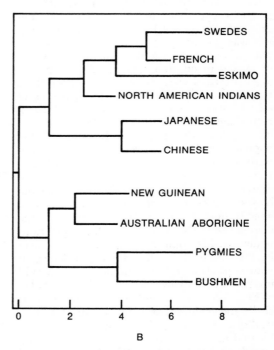

FIGURE 4.6. Diagrammatic representations of population distances and degrees of affinity based upon (A) groups of ten populations, measuring their separation from a common beginning on a scale proportional to the number of substitutions evident in fifty-eight genes, and (B) groups of ten comparable populations, using twenty-six external anthropometric measurements and observations. Note the different positions occupied by peoples of European descent in these two studies. From Luigi Luca Cavalli-Sforza, "The Genetics of Human Populations," **Scientific American** 231 (1974): 87.

adaptive responses to different ecological settings are the topics of these papers by a number of specialists in the field of human biology.

Boule, Marcellin and Vallois, Henri V. *Fossil Men*. New York: Dryden. 1957. While dated with respect to recent fossil man discoveries and conceptions of genetic distances between populations, this book is a valuable reference source on major sites of post-Pleistocene human occupation from which skeletal data have been taken.

Brues, Alice M. "The Maintenance of Genetic Diversity in Man." *Addison-Wesley Module in Anthropology* 42. 1973. The effects of cultural behavior upon the genetic constitution of human populations are discussed along with general principles of gene frequencies, selection, and polymorphisms in human groups.

Davis, Kingsley "The Migrations of Human Population," *Scientific American* 231 (1974):92-105. Prehistoric and historic movements of populations are reviewed in the light of recent studies of population genetics and demography.

Johnston, Francis, E. *Microevolution of Human Populations*. Englewood Cliffs, N.J.: Prentice-Hall, 1973. Similarities of microevolutionary processes operating in man and other mammalian species are noted, particular attention being given to the role of culture in channeling the course of human genetic variability over time.

Lasker, Gabriel G. "Human Biological Adaptability," *Science* 166 (1969):1480-1846. This is a good summary article of studies of climatic adaptations, disease frequencies in populations, and the goals of human geneticists in understanding gene activity in the context of the physical environment.

McCown, Theodore D. and Kennedy, Kenneth A. R., eds. *Climbing Man's Family Tree: A Collection of Major Writings on Human Phylogeny, 1699-1971*. Englewood Cliffs, N.J.: Prentice-Hall, 1972. The editors of this volume had prepared essays on the topic of human phylogeny as an intellectual concept in the natural sciences and anthropology. These essays introduce selections by various writers of phylogenetic theories.

Molnar, Stephen. *Races, Types and Ethnic Groups: the Problem of Human Variation*. Englewood Cliffs: Prentice-Hall, 1975. This valuable study of human variation has an important final chapter on the topic of "The Future of the Human Species."

Provine, William B. *The Origins of Theoretical Population Genetics*. Chicago: University of Chicago, 1971. The historical development of population genetics with interesting discussions of the personalities and backgrounds of major figures in the field is the focus of this very readable book.

Richardsen, Ken and Spears, David, eds. *Race, Culture and Intelligence*. New York: Penguin Books, 1972. This is a study of the nature of intelligence by nine authors in the fields of psychology, biology, and sociology. I.Q. Scores and other measures of intelligence are discussed.

Bibliography

Crawford, M. H. and P. L. Workman, eds. 1973. *Methods and Theories of Anthropological Genetics*. Albuquerque: University of New Mexico.

Dobzhansky, Theodosius. 1970. *The Genetics of the Evolutionary Process*. New York: Columbia University.

Kennedy, Kenneth A. R. 1965. "Human Skeletal Material from Ceylon with an Analysis of the Island's Prehistoric and Contemporary Populations," *Bulletin of the British Museum (Natural History)* 11:135-213.

———. 1972. "The Concept of the Vedda Phenotypic Pattern: Critical Analysis of Research on the Osteological Collections of a Remnant Population," *Spolia Zeylanica* 32:25-60.

———. 1974. "The Paleodemography of Ceylon: a Study of the Biological Continuum of a Population from Prehistoric to Historic Times," in *Perspectives in Palaeoanthropology*. ed., A. K. Ghosh Calcutta: Mukhopadhyay.

Oxnard, Charles 1973. *Form and Pattern in Human Evolution: Some Mathematical, Physical and Engineering Approaches*. Chicago: University of Chicago.

Rightmire, G. P. 1975. "Problems in the Study of Later Pleistocene Man in Africa," *American Anthropologist* 77:28-52.

5 | Human Diversity and the Modern World

NATIONALISTIC MOVEMENTS

The social philosophy asserting the importance of one nation over others whereby the policies of ethnic self-interest transcend concern for humanity is called *nationalism*. Its political and emotional roots are in the folk racism of all peoples. But nationalism involves more than an ethnocentric conviction of the natural superiority of one's own people and the inferiority of rivals: it is an attitude linked to imperialism, military aggression, and the formation of political states. Members of a nationalistic group are united by their devotion to a common language, an oral or literary tradition, a system of religious beliefs, a geographical territory, or to some other bond. These ties may enforce social sanctions for the exploitation of foreign peoples and the imposition of the victor's values and lifeways upon the conquered. Populations with little or no political power today may hold on to their "pride of race," an attitude enhanced in some cases by traditions of their descent from a nation of some political consequence in the past.

We find no difficulty in associating nationalistic movements with all of the major powers of the world today, but we can discern these too in the emerging political identities of Third World states in Africa and Asia. For almost two thousand years since the Romans dissolved the political autonomy of the Hebrew nation with its seat of government in Jerusalem, Jewish people have preserved their ethnic identity and their body of religious beliefs, a faith that contributed to the struggle to establish the modern state of Israel. But we would not attribute nationalistic behavior to Gypsies, even though they have hung on to their ethnic identity through centuries of persecution. At least these widely distributed people, originally from North India, have not sought to establish a Gypsy nation. Nor would the social philosophy of nationalism be applicable to many tribal populations isolated from major political states.

Nationalism is not a new phenomenon. Some of its elements are found in such widely separated areas of the world as pre-Columbian Meso-America, India, and China. Populations without a written language have pursued nationalistic goals, as did the inhabitants of various West African states prior to the time of European intervention. In the Western tradition, the Romans established an empire covering portions of three continents wherein Roman citizenship, with its devotion to duty to the state and its pride in Greco-Roman traditions, was a powerful cohesive force. With the fragmentation of the empire and the formation of feudal states in the Dark Ages, regional languages and customs developed rapidly. This political change led to individuals thinking of themselves as Saxons, Burgundians, or citizens of Florence rather than as citizens of Rome. The institutions of the church and the Holy Roman Empire provided a sense of continuity with the past, but by the sixteenth century new political federations had formed, the direct antecedents of modern European nations. New mercantile economic doctrines, the rise of a middle class, and a new genre in art and literature contributed to the establishment of nationalism of an order far more potent than ever before in history. The wars for independence in both North and South America and the consolidation of European petty states in reaction to Napoleonic aspirations are among the political consequences of the rising sense of self-determination in the Western world. By 1870 the more powerful European nations were extending their influence to colonizing and trading activities in Africa and Asia. The United States fought with Spain over the control of the Philippines in an imperialistic fling in the final years of the nineteenth century. Nationalistic movements in Germany have contributed to two global wars in this century. The chief task of world peace organizations today has been the reduction of the destructive effects of nationalistic movements in all countries.

It was inevitable that modern nationalism would add to its ideological arsenal the swords of racism. In the minds of many people, arguments for their nation's political superiority seemed inseparable from a demonstration of their racial superiority. Apart from the efforts of many scholars to investigate the nature of human variation without prejudicial attitudes and even to openly attack the racist doctrine that physical characters are inherently correlated with intellect and behavior, the very fact that men of science were investigating problems of human diversity at all lent an aura of scholarly respectability to certain racist claims. Add to the notion of scientific racism the ideas that people of European background are culturally and biologically more advanced than the inhabitants of other continents and the philosophies of nationalism and Social Darwinism, and the scene is set for the invention of racial mythologies by which nationalistic policies appear to be justifiable.

Aryanism, Celtism, and the myths of Slavic, Teutonic, and Anglo-Saxon superiority are those nationalistic superstitions that have brought forth the most prolific literature. But further examples are provided by writers of those minority populations that suffer from oppression by a politically dominant group and seek a sense of pride in their own cultural heritage.[1] Analagous efforts have been made by leaders of nationalistic movements who have turned to folklore, history, archeology, and racial anthropology to filter out elements sufficiently attractive to glorify the unique qualities of an *Irish race,* a *Nordic race,* a *Czech race,* an *American,* or a *Black race.* All nationalistic philosophies are characterized by mysticism, romanticism, and bad biology.

The racist myth that has most affected the modern world was born in the writings of Max Müller. In the 1860s, he identified ancient and contemporary speakers of Indo-European languages as members of an *Aryan* race. In 1888 Max Müller rejected his earlier belief that languages could be correlated with biological characters of their speakers.[2] However, the French statesman Arthur de Gobineau (1816-1882) had been putting together an aristocratic theory of Aryan origins as early as 1835 when he began his famous essay *The Inequality of Human Races.* This was published in 1855. Gobineau warned of the dangers of racial mixtures and cultural contaminations from non-Aryan populations. His idea that only the white race was culturally creative, and of this the Aryans were the finest, found a receptive audience among many readers of Max Müller's earlier works on Aryan language and race.[3]

Gobineau's ideas were taken up by German nationalists who formed an organization to perpetuate and spread his teachings. *Gobinism* was fundamental to the tenets of Nordic supremacy, which were forming by the dawn of World War I. Houston Stewart Chamberlain (1855-1927) was an Englishman who became a German citizen in order to preach without restraint his doctrine of Teutonic man's place at the top of the racial hierarchy. His book *Foundations of the Nineteenth Century* was published in 1890-1891, but many editions had appeared thereafter due to its tremendous

1. Malcolm X, *The Autobiography of Malcolm X* (New York: Grove, 1964), pp. 163-169.

2. Friedrich Max Müller, *Biographies of Words and the Home of the Aryas* (London: Green, 1888).

3. Adrian Collins, trans., *The Inequality of Human Races by Arthur de Gobineau* (New York: G. P. Putnam's Sons, 1915).

popularity.[4] No previous nationalist movement had the disasterous consequences of Adolf Hitler's (1889-1945) policies of mass execution and exile of so many millions of people. Yet genocide has continued in more recent years of this century in the U.S.S.R., Brazil, Southeast Asia, Africa, and elsewhere. Atrocities of this scope can occur with an oppressor's attitude of dehumanization of victims that is sanctioned by his society in the name of national honor. This behavior has been summarized by editors of a recent book on human aggression as follows:

Thus social destructiveness as we see it exhibits the following features: People do harm to other people or act in such a way as to sustain a pattern of harm. (Damage to things, in itself, is not included). Those who do the harm are forbidden to do it to a member of their own group. They act not separately on their individual initiative but with the permission or favor, or even under the command, of their group or leader or at least certain peers. They see the victims as less than human or falsely regard them as aggressive or both.[5]

The abuses of the race concept in modern politics led a number of scientists to favor an international convocation of experts to meet and seek agreement on the nature of race in the modern world. By 1950 the *UNESCO Statement by Experts on Race Problems* was issued under the sponsorship of the United Nations. Because the contributors meeting in Paris were largely selected from the social sciences and the ideas of biologists were not sufficiently represented, a second meeting was held the following year. This led to the publication of *Statement on the Nature of Race and Race Differences by Physical Anthropologists and Geneticists*. While these two statements contain more agreement than conflict between social scientists and their colleagues in the biological areas of research, two subsequent meetings were held in 1964 in Moscow and in 1967 in Paris. The final statement differs from those preceding it in its emphasis upon the causes of racism and how this destructive attitude can be combated by social and political actions on the part of all nations. Paragraph nineteen of this statement notes that

racial prejudice and discrimination in the world today arise from historical and social phenomena and falsely claim the sanction of science. It is, therefore, the responsibility of all biological and social scientists, philosophers, and others working in related disciplines, to ensure that the results of their research are not misused by those who wish to propagate racial prejudice and encourage discrimination.[6]

CHANGING CONCEPTS OF RACE

Through the fog of opinions that have prevailed for the past 200 years over the question of man's biological diversity, one landmark remained in sight: the idea that our species was divisible into natural entities. To Linnaeus these subspecific groupings were *varieties;* to his successors, the *races* of man. Disagreements arose over the identification of valid sorting criteria for classification, the effects of environment and (later, following the publication of the *Origin of Species*) of the effects of evolutionary mechanisms upon specific physical traits, the best methods for filtering from the present hodgepodge of racial crossings the characteristics of earlier pure racial lines, and the problem of what to do with individuals and populations who did not fit into the typological constructs of a well-ordered taxonomy. The fact that biologists concerned with subspecific taxa of species other than *sapiens* were seeking to establish racial taxonomies provided encouragement to the racial anthropologist that he too was on the right track, that the reality of race was irrefutable. Many anthropology textbooks in use today contain some form of racial classification, even though the authors of these books and the teachers who assign them may express reservations about the value of traditional race ideas as ap-

4. John Lees, trans., *Foundations of the Nineteenth Century by Houston Stewart Chamberlain* (London: Bodley Head, 1912).

5. Nevitt Sanford and Craig Comstock, eds., *Sanctions for Evil* (San Francisco: Jossey-Bass, 1971), p. 5.

6. M. F. Ashley Montagu, *Statement on Race: an Annotated Elaboration and Exposition of the Four Statements on Race Issued by the United Nations Educational, Scientific and Cultural Organization.* 3rd ed. (London: Oxford University, 1972).

plied to man. The UNESCO statements on race do not reject the validity of a race concept within the context of its biological and taxonomic limitations in classifying all living things.

Therefore it is of major significance in the study of human variation that there are a growing number of taxonomic biologists and anthropologists who say that the race concept has outlived its usefulness and finds no justification in modern biological research *on any species*. This is not a disclaimer of the importance of continuing research into the evolutionary phenomenon of variability, but it is a rejection of the practice of placing any group of organisms within subspecific divisions that are then regarded as *natural* components of a species. This new approach to race and variation raises some important questions, but perhaps we should discuss first why the race concept, viable only a few years ago and for so long a time in the history of science, is abandoned today. Some startling misconceptions about this matter persist in the popular media as well as within the discipline of anthropology.

One false idea is that taxonomy itself is suspect as a legitimate scientific effort, hence any classification of human groups will be devoid of meaning. This is not a denial of the concept of race, of course, but a rejection of any method for determining the frequencies and defining characters of naturally existing subdivisions of the species. Supporters of this bias have much to say about the arbitrary elements of all classifications in general and about the history of taxonomic error below the level of species in biology in particular.

Another misconception is that the race concept is being abandoned because it stands in the way of guaranteeing social equality to all ethnic groups. In other words, to say that races exist is to declare that one is a racist! For some people it has been a short step from this assumption to the conclusion that any study of the biological diversity in human populations is prejudicial to the welfare of all peoples. The historic coincidence of political tensions between members of different ethnic backgrounds, which was on the move in this country and abroad in the 1960s, with an anthropological disclaiming of the race concept

has contributed to the notion that the two events, political and scientific, are directly related. This notion is sometimes expressed as the idea that race was rejected by anthropologists when they perceived that the so-called scientific racial labels were merely reflections of popular racial classifications. Examples put forward to support this include the anthropological classifications of Irish populations at different periods of this group's upwardly moving social mobility over the past century in the United States, or the status of the minority population of the Eta of Japan.[7]

Finally, there is the often heard explanation that racial anthropology was given up because of the impossibility of ever separating out primeval lines of descent among contemporary populations which have become so thoroughly hybridized. This is the melting-pot theory wherein race per se is not denied, but hands are raised in despair in ever penetrating the past to discern the pure strains from whence all populations of the present were originally derived.

Now there are some grains of truth to each of these misconceptions, and any one or all of them have been instrumental in bringing about a change of mind for some individuals confused by the traditional notion of race. But we cannot accept these as being primary causes for a change in scientific opinion over the matter of race. The reason is that the factors contributing to modification of our thinking about human diversity and classification lie outside of anthropology and had emerged well before 1960.

As early as forty years ago, biologists studying variations in birds and insects began to perceive difficulties in classifying populations below the species level. Traditionally they had thought of subspecies or races as being genetically distinct and geographically separated groups, capable of interbreeding only in areas of contact. These populations were identified by Latin trinomials, and researchers ventured forth to discover new subspecies. This practice was particularly prevalent in fields of biology

7. Gloria A. Marshall, "Racial Classifications: Popular and Scientific," *Science and the Concept of Race,* ed. Margaret Mead, *et al.* (New York: Columbia University, 1968, 149-164).

where a high proportion of major species groups had been described and named already. At one time in the not too distant past, a total of thirty-five races of the pocket gopher *Thomomys battae* and *T. talpoides* had been identified in Utah alone. Subspecies of some insect species were named in the hundreds.

Since all subspecies are potentially interfertile, classification below the species level was established upon comparisons of selected phenotypic characters and by relative degree of geographical separation of populations. Then questions arose as to the arbitrary nature of sorting criteria. Single phenotypic characters were seldom cited in the tracing of a presumed biological continuum. One investigator discovered in 1940 that the number of races counted in his study of *Lymantria dispar,* a moth species, increased as a function of the number of traits considered in his study.[8] Might not populations of the same species evolve new characters in time without undergoing division into subspecies and ultimately into new species? In fact we know this does happen.

At the time biologists were becoming sensitive to the fact that a considerable degree of subjectivity was involved in recognizing new subspecies by observation of one or a few diagnostic features, it appeared too that these features were not genetically linked. Rather, a given population possesses varying frequencies of discrete, independent characters that form new associations in the microevolutionary history of the gene pool and show independent geographical correlations. So it was that taxonomists working outside the field of human genetics and the anthropological race concept came to recognize that discordant variation is the rule for all species, and the assumption of coordinated variation was insupportable.

In 1944 another investigator of the subspecies question plotted a dozen so-called racial criteria for three geographical groups of *Rana pipiens,* the common leopard frog of eastern North America. He did not observe any clustering of these traits over the broad geographical range of the species. Instead, he found gradual clines, step clines, and mid-distribution cline reversals for each trait included in his study. The axes of the clines lay along different compass orientations. This research confirmed the existence of discordant variation and thus pointed out the futility of drawing racial maps with sharp boundaries or even with zones of racial contact. The author of this study concluded that, "there is no generally accepted and easily applied criterion for recognizing subspecies."[9]

In the light of these considerations, it became evident to taxonomic biologists that no true lower limit of subspecies category could be established. All degrees of difference are observable in populations, some showing obvious differentiation by a number of characters while other populations appear to be distinctive by the presence of a single character. Frustrated by this impass to straightforward classification, some taxonomists proposed a level of statistical reliability that came closest to their personal notion of what would constitute a race in a particular biotic group. For example, one researcher decided that if 84 percent of the characters he selected for a species of bird called the Pacific petrel were shared by two petrel populations, these were to be considered members of the same race. But his critics quite properly pointed out that his method was arbitrary. Why had he settled on that particular statistical value?[10]

To this list of problems perceived by biologists of the subspecies concept others may be added. The list could include (1) the rates of evolutionary change, which are responsive to the mechanisms of natural selection, mutation, gene migration, and drift, vary in different population and in a single population at different periods of time—a fact formerly passed over; (2) the appearance of similar phenotypic characters in seemingly unrelated populations may be due to parallelism and not to any genetic affinity; (3) the genetic basis for phenotypic criteria used in the classification of

8. Richard Goldschmidt, *The Material Basis of Evolution* (New Haven, Conn.: Yale University, 1940).

9. John Alexander Moore, "Geographic Variation in *Rana pipiens* Schreber of Eastern North America," *Bulletin of the American Museum of Natural History* 82 (1944):349-369.

10. Oliver Luther Austin, "Notes on Some Petrels of the North Pacific," *Bulletin of the Museum of Comparative Zoology* 107 (1952):391-407.

races is little known about, hence it is impossible to determine the effects of environmental factors on the phenotypic expressions observed: (4) the identification of subspecies has been based upon a finite number of criteria, the evolutionary significance of which was also imperfectly understood; (5) finally, biologists came to see that the model of species—a closed genetic system of reproductive isolates—had been employed inappropriately in a classification of populations below the species level, populations with open genetic systems where genes come into a population by hybridization as well as by mutative factors in the genes and chromosomes.

In 1948 the Commission of Zoological Nomenclature, meeting in Paris, continued its sanction of named subspecies, while putting minor categories without geographical connotation, such as *breed* and *variety* an inferior rank. This was considered to be a mistake by many biologists, a needless retention of a traditional taxonomic entity that had been laid to rest already by researchers actively involved in the subspecies problem. One objector to the Commission's procedure had already made this statement in 1946:

The use of subspecific names not only implies discontinuity where none may exist, but also unity where there may be, in fact, discontinuity. . . . Certainly in the case of *Erithracus rubecula* (a European robin) it is both simpler and more accurate to describe subspecific variation in terms of geographical trends, and omit altogether the tyranny of subspecific names.[11]

All this happened in the thirties, forties, and fifties well outside the realm of anthropological preoccupation with the classification of man. By the late 1950s several anthropologists became sufficiently aware of this literature on the subspecies problem to recognize that every objection to a race concept that had been applied to plants and animals was equally relevant to *Homo sapiens*.[12] A few years later in the pages of the scientific journal *Current Anthropology*[13] and in articles contributed to a volume on race edited by Montagu[14] the real historical roots of anthropology's rejection of the race concept are to be found. A comparison of anthropological approaches to the race concept with those we have been discussing in the sphere of biological taxonomy will be useful in understanding why the majority of modern scholars in both fields are in agreement today over the key issues of subspecies taxonomy.

One common obstacle to racial classification of human and nonhuman species is the arbitrary nature of selecting sorting criteria. From the time of Herodotus's accounts of ancient populations to the days when Pearson's Coefficient of Racial Likeness came into fashion, descriptive data for human groups have been biased by the selective factor in making use of phenotypic characters easy to observe. Even with the invention of anthropometric procedures and use of genetic variables, the question of the relative evolutionary importance of sorting criteria remains with us. Is the color of the skin a better or a worse indicator of an individual's population than the features of his blood chemistry? Should the cephalic index be preferred over pharmacogenetic responses?

As was discovered in the study of phenotypic variation in frogs, so the anthropologist finds in the species of his major interest: biological characters selected as sorting criteria for subspecific classification do not form natural clusters or linkages. Long noses grace long faces as well as broad faces. Not all blue-eyed people have flaxen hair, demand a piece of candy after experiencing a PTC test, are heterozygous for the MN blood group system, or are free from the incidence of Tay-Sachs dis-

11. David Lack, "The Taxonomy of the Robin *Erithracus rubecula* (Linn.)," *Bulletin of the British Ornithological Club* 66 (1946):55-65.

12. *Cold Spring Harbor Symposium on Quantitative Biology: Genetics and Twentieth Century Darwinism* 24 (1959).

13. Frank B. Livingstone, "On the Non-Existence of Human Races," *Current Anthropology* 3 (1962): 279; Theodosius Dobzhansky, "Comments on Livingstone," *Current Anthropology* 3 (1962):279-280, W. Wiercinski, "The Racial Analysis of Human Populations in Relation to their Ethnogenesis," *Current Anthropology* 3 (1962):9-20; Marshall T. Newman, "Geographic and Micrographic Races," *Current Anthropology* 5 (1963):189-207; and Jean Hiernaux, "Comments on Newman," *Current Anthropology* 4 (1963):198-199.

14. M. F. Ashley Montagu, ed., *The Concept of Race* (New York: Free Press, 1964).

ease in their population. The concept of discordant variation is clearly illustrated in figure 5.1 here. The same idea may be demonstrated by comparing one map of a geographical region that depicts different mean values for a trait—let's say, the frequency of stature variables—with a second map of the same region showing the mean frequencies of another trait —for example, the sickle-cell gene. It is highly unlikely that you would be able to establish a good geographical correlation for these two in-

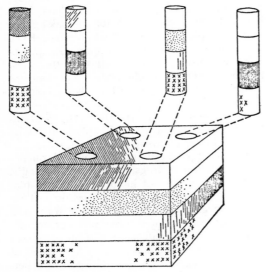

FIGURE 5.1. Diagram of discordant variation in four characters. Each layer of the cube represents the geographical variation of a particular biological character. For example, if the top layer represents skin color, individuals in the near left-hand corner would have the darkest skins, those on the right-hand side of the cube would have lighter skins, etc. Cores are extracted from the cube which represent samples of individuals from a geographical area. Each sample is different, so we might say each one was a **race.** However, a set of four samples taken at any four places in the cube would also produce four different races. There is no natural racial division because the geographical variations are discordant. From Paul R. Ehrlich and Richard W. Holm, **The Concept of Race.** M. F. Ashley Montagu, ed. New York: Free Press, 1964, p. 170, fig. 3.

dependent variables. The plotting of additional phenotypic characters on other maps that could be laid over these two would emphasize all the more that individuals inhabiting a region do not all share identical genetic constitutions. Identity of this level occurs only in monozygotic twins, and even with these individuals nongenetic variations are present.

Boundaries drawn on a map represent focal areas of presumed racial distribution, but they do not reflect the actual state of things in nature. What appears in a map of trait distributions is a clinal or gradient pattern. The cline of each trait under consideration has its own unique configuration. Statements that populations are assignable to one race or another on the basis of sharing a certain percentage of phenotypic traits are invalid, for different traits have different and unrelated clinal patterns.

Difficulty in establishing rates of evolutionary change for different populations as well as learning that evolutionary mechanisms have been operative in the course of the biological history of a population present other limits to the acceptance of a race concept for man. Might the present distribution of blood type B in Europe be due to the prehistoric migrations of Asiatic peoples from regions where this gene occurs in high frequency today? Or is the frequency of the gene due to mutation or selection? Is the absence of the B gene in pre-Columbian America due to genetic drift or to natural selection?

Of course many of the problems we face in attempting to answer questions like these are related to our ignorance of the genetic basis of many human phenotypic characters. Therefore it becomes impossible to understand the way many traits develop over a range of different ecological settings. We recognize that there are individual alterations in stature measurements that are related to conditions of our nutrition, fatigue, psychological stress, and perhaps to cultural practices as well. Certainly these factors affect our interpretations of variability within and between populations. While we can appreciate the adaptive factors of body form and size in Arctic and East African populations, we do not understand the polygenic constitutions for these differences. Such variables would make poor criteria for a racial taxonomy if the latter represented something real in nature.

Today we know that the existence of a similar physical character in two or more widely separated populations is not a *de facto* revelation of biological affinity, as some early racial anthropologists had assumed. Rather it may be attributed to evolutionary parallelism. However, like-characters in separate populations are not necessarily the result of the same evolutionary mechanisms. We may explain the prominence of cheek bones in the faces of some populations living in cold climate zones as a part of the thermal adaptation of selective advantage in their habitat. But prominent cheek bones appear among some tropical forest peoples of South America as well. Is this an example of parallelism whereby facial structures have evolved under different environmental situations or is it a single trait of common origin reflecting an ancestral bond of native Americans to cold-adapted Asiatics? Spiral hair form and dark skin pigmentation are features that occur in high frequency in sub-Saharan Africa and in Melanesia, but is the term *Oceanic Negroids* still appropriate in referring to Melanesian populations?

Students of human variation ceased to ad-

vance a race concept when they perceived, as had their colleagues in animal taxonomy, that efforts to define a *type* for subspecies were as unrealistic as the habit of thinking that interfertile populations could be divided into categories as though these populations were closed genetic systems, as are species. Inhibitions to speciation in *Homo sapiens* may be as ancient as the human family itself for at least most of the period of the Pleistocene.[15]

How are we to discuss problems of human variation without reference to the term *race*, even when this four-letter word is stripped of its connotations with typology, subspecific taxonomy, and racism? For some anthropologists the attempt would be impossible, and they propose alternate terms that are not encumbered with emotional and outmoded meanings: *ethnic group, polytype,* and the like. Garn suggests that we be mindful of the misuses of the term *race,* but continue to employ it in a more precise way, as in distinguishing *local race,* corresponding to the breeding population, from *geographical race,* which means a collection of populations sharing a number of phenotypic characters.[16]

An identical problem is discussed by two taxonomists who are not anthropologists or concerned in the context of their paper with the term race as applied to man:

Thus, in publications, we can speak of '*Rana pipiens* Schreber, Montauk Point, New York', or '*R. pipiens,* southeastern corner of J. B. Smith farm, 5 miles west of Montauk Point, in cattail swamp'; or even '*R. pipiens* from Long Island' . . . 'from the East Coast', and so on. . . Inevitably, perhaps, repeatedly discussed populations will come to be referred to as 'Mantauk A', 'Reelfoot Lake', 'Rock Island', and so forth, but this will no more prove a pitfall than is the geographical vernacular familiarly applied to 'strains' of *Drosophila virilis* . . ., or the locality names by which experienced trappers can often distinguish a series of pelts.[17]

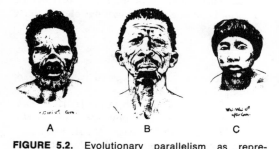

A   B   C

FIGURE 5.2. Evolutionary parallelism as represented by very broad noses (platyrrhiny) in individuals from three widely separated populations from (A) northern Australia, (B) southwestern Africa, and (C) eastern Peru. Note the variations in hair form, shape of the eye opening, cranial robusticity, and shape of the face. These morphological features occur in relatively high frequencies in the populations to which these individuals belong. Drawn from photographs in the collections of the British Museum of Natural History, London, by Rosemary Powers.

15. Kenneth A. R. Kennedy, "The Paleontology of Human Populations," *The Biologist* 54 (1972):97-114.

16. Garn, *Human Races,* p. 9.

17. Edward O. Wilson and William L. Brown, "The Subspecies Concept and Its Taxonomic Applications," *Systematic Zoology* 2 (1953):97-111.

MAN'S FUTURE

Any effort to predict the biological future of our species must be viewed through the lens of those concepts about human variation that have developed over many centuries in the Western world. To be sure, we have moved away from a typological conception of man's diversity into areas of research devoted to the clarification of evolutionary processes in populations. We now recognize that the biochemical units of inheritance are manifested in a great variety of ways under different ecological settings. And we have a greater appreciation than before of human adaptability to physical and cultural targets of selection.

Apart from popular myths about our brains getting bigger and our teeth getting smaller, and fewer, it appears that human biological diversity will be shaped most significantly by the effects of a greater degree of gene migration than has been the case in the past, and that selective pressures of greatest consequence will come through the effects of overpopulation, pollution, and the threat of global wars. For some fifteen million years, members of the human family have adapted to a tremendous range of ecological settings imposed by the physical and cultural environments, and this reflection may give us hope that *Homo sapiens* may adapt to new circumstances presented by his surroundings. It is the rapidity with which new selective pressures appear and our uncertainty as to the limitations of human variability and adaptability that preclude complacency about the future.

Certainly man is unique among the other living things on this planet in his capacity to control a wider range of phenomena in his environment. The mechanism for this control is cultural behavior, our species' most critical adaptive specialization. It is transferred not through the genes but through the training and experiences of individual men and women. What is there in the nonhuman world to compare to a Confusius, a Charles Darwin, a Johann Sebastian Bach? Or, for that matter, an Adolf Hitler or a future Dr. Strangelove who really will reshuffle humanity's gene pool?

Our hope for survival as a species rests not only in summit meetings and *détente*: upon the values we place on understanding the potentials and limitations of human diversity depends our course of ongoing evolution. An eminent geneticist has written, "Ethics are . . . a human responsibility. We cannot rely on genes or on natural selection to guarantee that man will always choose the right direction of his evolution."[18]

For Further Reading

Brace, C. Loring and Livingstone, Frank B. "On Creeping Jensenism," *Warner Modular Populations* 295 (1973):1-12. Two anthropologists discuss the anthropological implications of the work of Arthur R. Jensen and the idea that intelligence is determined most directly by genes.

Poliakov, Leon *The Aryan Myth: a History of Racist and Nationalist Ideas in Europe.* New York: Basic Books. 1971. An historian of anti-Semitism traces the origins and progress of the Aryan myth in political contexts in Western culture. This is a good source book for major writings on race and nationalism.

Snyder, Louis L. *The Idea of Racialism: Its Meaning and History.* Princeton: D. Van Nostrand, 1962. This is a study of the fallacy of scientific racism, including parts of writings of over thirty authors.

Bibliography

Bateson, Gregory 1974. *Steps to an Ecology of Mind.* New York: Ballantine.

Ehrlich, Paul R. and Ehrlich, Anne H. 1970. *Population, Resources, Environment: Issues in Human Ecology.* San Francisco: W. H. Freeman.

Lerner, I. Michael 1968. *Heredity, Evolution and Society.* San Francisco: W. H. Freeman.

Murdoch, William W. 1975. *Environment: Resources, Pollution and Society,* 2d ed. Sunderland, Mass.: Sinauer Associates.

Spuhler, J. N., ed. 1967. *Genetic Diversity and Human Behavior.* Chicago: Aldine.

18. Theodosius Dobzhansky, *The Biological Basis of Human Freedom* (New York: Columbia University Press, 1960), p. 134.

Glossary

Anthropometry—The technique of measuring the human body with respect to dimensions, ratios, proportions, and qualitative descriptions of morphological features.

Biological Continuum—Lineage of a group of related organisms considered in the context of evolutionary changes over a period of time.

Chain of Being—The concept that all natural phenomena can be arranged in an hierarchical order from simplest to most complex forms; the *Scala naturae* or Ladder of Being.

Chromosome—The fibrous structure carrying the linear arrangements of genes in the cell nucleus. The number of chromosomes is species-specific, man having forty-six.

Cline—A gradual change in the frequency of a phenotypic character of a population of related organisms across the range of their geographical distribution; a gradient of a variable biological trait.

Deme—A local interbreeding population; the basic evolutionary unit.

Discordant Variation—Independent expression of discrete phenotypic characters in a species or population.

Discriminant Function—A statistical measure of the degree of difference between two sets of variables.

Eugenics—Study of how physical and mental characters of real or assumed genetic basis can be improved for the human species by the practice of selective mating.

Founder Effect—Formation of a new population by one or more individuals from a larger population. Such founders may be genetically related, but their genetic contribution is limited and unrepresentative of the gene pool from which they were derived.

Gene—An hereditary unit at a given chromosome locus; a giant molecule of nucleoprotein deoxyribonucleic acid (DNA).

Gene Flow—Migration of genes from one population into another or mutual exchange of genetic material between two or more populations; the genetic consequence of hybridization or interbreeding and intermating.

Gene Pool—All genetic material contained in an interbreeding population that is actually or potentially transferable to a succeeding generation.

Genetic Drift—A random change in gene frequencies in a population, an effect that is greatest in small and isolated populations.

Genotype—An individual's genetic constitution.

Heterozygosity—Possession, in the genotype, of two different forms of a gene at corresponding loci on a pair of homologous chromosomes.

Hominid—The taxonomic family of primates that includes man and fossil species related to him. Latin—*Hominidae*.

Homozygosity—Possession, in the genotype, of the same forms of a gene at corresponding loci on a pair of homologous chromosomes.

Microevolution—Gradual and small effect evolutionary changes occurring over populational generations.

Monogenesis—The theory that a group of related organisms are descendants of a common ancestor.

Mosaic Chronology—Estimation of the date of creation to some six thousand years ago on the basis of geneological data contained in the first five books of the Bible. Authorship of the *Pentateuch* has been ascribed to Moses.

Mutation—A random change in the constitution of genetic material that may be expressed in the sudden appearance of a novel phenotypic character.

Natural Selection—Differential survival of those organisms possessing biological traits that are most adaptive for producing offspring; the failure of less well endowed organisms to survive and transfer their traits to the next generation. This is a natural mechanism of evolutionary change to be distinguished from artificial selection (breeding experimentation) and supernatural intervention (Providentialism).

Parallelism—Independent evolution of a similar phenotypic character in two evolutionary lines after their divergence from an earlier common ancestor. Similar adaptive traits may arise from the effects of similar environmental pressures operating upon both groups of organisms.

Phenotype—The physical or behavioral manifestations that are the sum total of the effects of the interaction between an individual's genotype and the environment.

Phylogeny—Evolutionary relationships among organisms; the origin and evolution of taxonomic categories.

Polygenesis—The theory that a group of apparently similar organisms have fundamental biological and behavioral differences that denote descent along separate ancestral lines.

Polygenic Variable—A phenotypic character that is the expression of the interaction of discrete genes at different loci on one or several chromosomes, as distinguished from phenotypic expression due to single gene inheritance.

Polymorphism—More than one phenotypic expression of a biological or behavioral character within a species or population; a trait controlled by two or more genes on the same locus of homologous chromosomes that determine alternative phenotypic characters.

Polytypism—The concept that a species is represented by populations of more than one kind, such as a variety or race, in different localities of its geographical range.

Preadaptation—The evolutionary phenomenon that pertains to the appearance of a phenotypic change in a group of organisms that may be of no immediate benefit in the environment in which the population is living, but may become important for survival and so increase in frequency if the population encounters another and different environment at a subsequent time.

Primitivism—Philosophical speculations as to the origins and lifeways of primeval man.

Sexual Selection—The concept of preferential mating whereby individual organisms with the greater ability to attract mates will be the major contributors to the gene pools of their population by leaving the highest number of progeny best suited for survival.

Social Darwinism—The philosophy defined by Spencer that society functions as an organism and is responsive to a deterministic mechanism analagous to natural selection whereby the "free play of the fit" should be recognized in legal and political endeavors.

Species—The taxonomic category below the genus representing a group of closely related organisms capable of interbreeding and producing fertile offspring, but remaining reproductively isolated from other species.

Taxonomy—The science of classification of living things; systematics.

Zygote—The cell resulting from the fusion of male and female gametes (ovum and sperm cell) at the time of fertilization.

Index

heterozygosity, 50, 52, 83
Hippocrates, 10-11
Hitler, Adolf, 76, 82
Hobbes, Thomas, 20
Holy Roman Empire, 75
Homa shell mound, 67
Home, Henry (Lord Kames), 1, 33
Homer, 8-9
Hominidae, 83
Homo erectus, 45, 60-62, 69. *See* Pithecanthropus.
Homo sapiens
    antiquity of, 18, 28, 44-45, 60-72
    Linnaean classification of, 24-28
homozygosity, 50, 52, 83
Hooton, Earnest Albert, 59
Howells, William W., 58-59
Hrdlička, Aleš, 43
humanism, 20-22
Hunter, John, 27
Hutton, James, 38
Huxley, Thomas Henry, 42, 45-46, 61

Ichthyophagi, the, 8
inheritance of acquired characteristics
    Blumenbach's concept of, 26-27
    E. Darwin's concept of, 36
    Herodotus's concept of, 7
    Hippocrates's concept of, 10-11
    Weismann's concept of, 48
International Biological Program, 70-71
I.Q. tests, 60
Isidore of Seville, 16-17
Isocrates, 7

Jensen, Arthur R., 60
Jews, the, 1, 8, 71
Jones, William, 44

Kant, Immanuel, 31, 36
Khartum, 67
Kourounkorokale, 67
Kulturkreis school, 64

lactase deficiency, 58
Lamarck, Jean Baptist Pierre Antoine de Monet de,
    36-37, 42
language
    Aryan, 44, 68
    cultural barriers of, 54
    nationalism and, 74-76
    Tower of Babel and, 15, 33
La Peyrére, Isaac de, 19
Lapps, the, 71
Lawrence, William, 30-31, 33, 36
Linnaeus, Carolus, 23-26, 76
Livingstone, Frank, 59
Lucretius, 10, 12

Lybians, 8
Lyell, Charles, 37-39, 46

Macrocephali, the, 8, 11
malaria, 59
Malthus, Thomas, 39-40
Mapungubue, 67
Marco Polo, 16
Maupertuis, Pierre Louis Moreau de, 31, 36
Max Müller, Friedrich, 63, 75-76
Meier, Albert, 18
meiosis, 50
melanin, 57
Mendel, Gregor, 40-41, 48, 55
Mendelians, the, 48
Mesolithic, the, 65-72
microevolution, 52, 58-59, 66, 83
migrations, 8, 15-16, 18-19, 28, 44-45, 60-72. *See*
    gene flow.
mitosis, 50
monogenesis, 16, 18-19, 28-35, 84
monsters
    Blumenbach rejects concept of, 26-27
    Homo monstrosus Linn., 25
    Greco-Roman concepts of, 8-14
    medieval concepts of, 15-16, 21-22
Montaigne, Michel de, 19
Morgan, Henry Lewis, 49
Morton, Samuel, 27, 32
Mosaic chronology, 14, 20, 37-38
Mount Carmel, 67
Muenster, Sebastian, 17
Muge, 66
multivariate analysis, 70
Mussolini, Benito, 1
mutation
    adaptive, 53
    evolutionary significance of, 48, 52-53, 71, 80, 83
    Lawrence's concept of, 30-31
    Mendelian, 48
    Prichard's concept of, 29-30
    rates of, 79

nationalism, 74-76
Natufians, the, 67
natural selection
    C. Darwin's concept of, 35-43
    evolutionary significance of, 54-56, 71, 78, 80, 84
    pre-Darwinian, 30, 32
Neanderthal man, 44-45, 60-62, 68-69
Neolithic, the, 59, 65-72
Ngandong, 69
Niah, 60, 69
Nott, Josiah Clark, 33-35

Ofnet, 66

Paleolithic, the, 65-70
parallelism, evolutionary, 70, 78, 81, 84